BETWEEN THE SHORE AND THE CITY

THE CITY

Tragedy at Mays Landing

MARI D'ALBORA DATTOLO

Dedicated to my 'spirited'
5th grade teacher,
Mr. John J. Williams.

*"Never underestimate
your Power to
Make A Difference."*

When the Rails ruled the Roads
and Class determined Privilege.

PREFACE

Growing up at the Jersey Shore, more specifically, Toms River, N.J., I spent my summers around the Boardwalks in the Central and Southern parts of the state. I worked at the pork roll stand in Seaside Heights and learned to embrace "midweek" weekends. Culturally, historically, economically, and socially we had the best of both worlds. Tourism in New Jersey was thriving in the 1980s, and there was no shortage of rewarding opportunities that opened up with each new casino, just an hour down our shores.

My career in the hospitality industry began in 1982 with the 'new' *Atlantic City Tropicana Hotel Casino*. Decades in the field included: hotels, airlines, event planning and restaurant marketing, including a period with *Trinity Irish Pub*. In 2009, I was at the peak of my career as my two daughters were preparing to leave the nest. I was 47 years old when Parkinson's Disease showed up on my doorstep.

Next Chapter:

I launched a historical travel series and became editor for *Jersey Shore Family* magazine, rebuilding the website for our local Historical Society. It was in that capacity that I uncovered the 1880 Train Tragedy, having been long forgotten. As a lifelong student of New Jersey History and a decades-long Mays Landing resident, I was intrigued by our hometown story and our contribution to the Second

Industrial Revolution. In my research as an investigative journalist, I began a fascinating journey of historic discovery. Persons and places connected with this story have their roots in Millville, Philadelphia, Camden, Florence, Atlantic City, and eventually lead right back to the accident scene, where it all happened in Mays Landing.

As I continued my research, I found that my imagination was sparked just as much as my curiosity. What were these people like? What did they do with their time before it was taken away from them by tragedy? While recording the facts behind the research, the humanity behind the statistics began to emerge.

What you are about to read is not only the account of my investigative journalism, but my best attempts to bring these people to life. All dialogue in this book, unless otherwise stated, is a dramatization based on my research. I sincerely hope that the blend of fact and imagination will provoke your interest and empathy as much as it did mine.

The following account includes excerpts from actual regional newspapers that recorded the events surrounding the Mays Landing tragedy. In 1880, as with our media today, news reports were dependent on a reliable communication system. With the newly developed transcontinental telegraph, word of this event reached national news outlets within minutes of being released. The following compilation of 19th-century reporting and 20th-century research provides a look into how this story unfolded over 140 years ago.

Warning: Some readers may find the graphic details of the following account to be disturbing.

ATLANTIC CITY N·J·

AMERICA'S GREATEST
ALL-THE-YEAR-ROUND RESORT
THROUGH VIA-
PENNSYLVANIA RAILROAD
DELAWARE RIVER BRIDGE ROUTE-

❧ I ❧

Among New Jersey's many treasures is the Great Egg Harbor
River National Park, running through Atlantic County's seat of
Mays Landing. Stretching 55 miles, this picturesque river meanders
through much of the Pinelands National Reserve, draining over 308
square miles of wetlands into the Atlantic Ocean. The Great Egg
Harbor River earned its name after the abundance of eggs laid by
nesting shorebirds. Immersed in these waters is a long-forgotten,
tragic tale of the human cost of industry and progress in our young
country's history.

In 1740, Captain George May, a surveyor and agent for the West
Jersey Society, sailed up the Great Egg Harbor River and found the
area ideal for shipbuilding. From 1830 to 1880, lumber from the area's
dense forests of pine and oak was used to build more than 200 vessels.

GREAT EGG HARBOR RIVER, MAYS LANDING

By the end of the century, wooden shipbuilding began to disappear as rail lines became the primary source of transportation over long distances. It was the dawn of a new era and a time of corporate supremacy in America's Second Industrial Age. This quiet town of Mays Landing would witness the single deadliest event in its history in the summer of 1880. Only in recent years have the layers of this tragedy been peeled away to reveal a much deeper truth.

THE SECOND INDUSTRIAL REVOLUTION COMES TO SOUTH JERSEY

Richard D. Wood V, a West Jersey Quaker, saw the economic advantage of southern New Jersey's seasonal resorts and abundant natural resources. He and six business partners met in 1845 to consider "a continuous railway to connect Philadelphia with the Great West." Richard was heavily involved in promoting and trading stocks of railroad companies, as well as the interests of the Schuylkill Navigation Company in Philadelphia. He would become an organizer and director of the Pennsylvania Railroad (PRR) and one of the most successful businessmen of his time.

Founded in 1846, the PRR was headquartered in Philadelphia with an eventual workforce of 250,000. The PRR grew to become the largest publicly traded corporation in the world.

Development of a regional rail system began in Pennsylvania in 1854 with a line west from Philadelphia to Pittsburgh. From there, the Transcontinental Railroad would expand to a national line with the meeting of the Central Pacific and Union Pacific Railroads in Promontory, Utah, in 1869, completing a six-year cross-country effort. With the coordination of the railroad network came the expansion to a national communications line. The alliance of the eastern and western coasts by telegraph enabled news of the merger of the two railroads in Utah to reach Washington DC within moments. Information sent via telegraph through Western Union would also allow the news media and government agencies to share information more efficiently. Furthermore, the emergence of the telegraph would give rise to the first wire news service, the Associated Press, enabling breaking news, like a fatal train collision, to reach news outlets in 37 states and seven territories within minutes.

Having sharpened his business prowess, Richard D. Wood V began negotiations with the New Jersey State Legislature to build a regional rail line. The new WJ&A would offer passenger service to shore points while also moving his textile goods. Rail lines would connect Philadelphia with routes south to Woodbury, Glassboro, Bridgeton, Millville, and eventually shore towns, including Atlantic City. In addition to trains as a shipping option to the country's interior cities, R.D. Wood & Co. would also utilize their fleet of schooners and sloops for trade with coastal cities in Eastern ports.

In Camden, the PRR was the strong arm over shore and inland traffic. Ownership of the ferry system and riverfront properties became theirs, giving the PRR the authority to reroute streets and determine traffic patterns, as well as the power to dictate the city's factory locations. Following an old Quaker route to cross the Delaware River from Philadelphia to Camden, the ferry-to-rail connection made same-day round-trip travel to New Jersey's shore points possible. Years later, the development of the Delaware Bridge-later renamed the Ben Franklin Bridge, connected the two northeast Quaker cities of Philadelphia and Camden.

In 1880, a new Ferry House was constructed at the foot of Wood Street in Camden, affectionately referred to as *"Philadelphia's Front Door to Atlantic City,"* to accommodate the growing rail service. The unique

3

fleet of two-story packet boats were steam-driven ferries consisting of a coal-burning steam boiler for propulsion and a rudder attached at each end for maneuverability on the opposite shore. The main deck transported freight, horse-drawn vehicles, as well as produce and livestock from South Jersey farms to markets in Philadelphia.

A FAMILY AFFAIR

Wood took ownership of Millville Iron Works with 20,000 acres of land, formerly belonging to his step brother, David Cooper Wood, when it went up for sheriff's sale in 1850. With the development of Millville, Richard dramatically increased production capacity and expanded the company's holdings. Thereafter, he would address ownership of his businesses as R.D. Wood & Co. Wood was not only the driving force behind what would become the City of Millville; he was also largely responsible for getting the Millville and Glassboro Railroad launched. Within the year, he began enlarging the Maurice River canal in Millville to meet the increasing demand for water power by the various mills. His investments in various Pennsylvania mines assured him a steady supply of iron and coal while planning the construction the New Jersey Mills was underway. The developed Millville site contained grist mills, sawmills, a cotton mill, glassworks, bleach and dye works.

In 1866, Richard's son, George Wood, traveled to England to purchase equipment and hire skilled operators for their growing enterprise. Cotton milling would be the first industry to streamline operations by utilizing automatic machinery. Edmund Cartwright is credited with inventing a loom powered by water turbines. After witnessing their value, Wood opened trade with city waterworks and mills throughout New England. R.D. Wood & Co. sought approval from the state legislature in 1868 to have a three and a half mile pond constructed to power their South Jersey mills. Covering 1,100 acres with a 24-foot fall, Union Lake retains the distinction of being the largest artificial lake in the state of New Jersey. In later reflections, Richard, Sr., considered the Maurice River Dam to be his crowning achievement.

COTTON MILL OF THE MAYS LANDING WATER POWER CO., MAYS LANDING, N. J.

Cotton Mill
of the Mays Landing Water Power Co.

Upon the mill's success, exported goods reached ports in Cuba, Puerto Rico, Turkey, and the Philippines. By that time, the daily intake of raw cotton had reached a demand of 11,000 pounds a day. In years to come, they became the only textile plant in New Jersey to take in raw cotton for processing. The Mays Landing Water Power Company, owned by R.D. Wood & Co., was the second cotton mill built by the Wood's in New Jersey. In addition to the cotton mill that produced toweling and fabrics, they also built modest company-owned housing as well as a one-room schoolhouse for children in the mill's employ. Furthermore, the company provided the Mays Landing General Store[1] and established a credit program for employees to borrow against their wages.

The mill had its own currency that enabled employees to buy nearly any staple needed for subsistence, even including an on-site coal yard. When the mill opened in 1865, it immediately became the town's largest employer, providing work for nearly a quarter of its residents. In 1880, the cotton mill employed 42 men, 57 women, and 29 children, doubling that number in less than a decade. The mills and mill towns

5

were the private property of the management, giving them the power to terminate leases and evict workers from their homes at will. Debts that were owed after buying merchandise on credit could be called in at any time. The system also prevented workers from accumulating capital in the form of home equity. As a result, a job loss would not only be tragic for the wage earner but also devastating for his entire family.

With the "Factory Act" in 1833, owners who had working children in their employ were required to provide a minimum of two hours of schooling every day, thereby explaining the location of the company's schoolhouse within a block of the mill. Employees of the Wood mills worked a 10.25 hour day, six days a week. Additionally, from 1920 and beyond, the Mays Landing Water Power Company would be the sole provider of the town's electricity. Each evening, the electricity was shut down at a specific time, giving the company control over their work-force's public and private hours.

Once the Millville Manufacturing Company was incorporated, foundry operations were expanded to a new site in Florence. Located on the Delaware River north of Philadelphia, the city factory had also fallen into bankruptcy. The company produced water and gas pipes, fire hydrants, valves, and other cast iron products marketed in both the U.S. and Europe. In his commitment to support those in his employ, Richard, Sr., considered housing developments, recreational facilities, stores, and a library for his mill workers. Today, several of the water and sewer systems constructed in Florence during those years are still in operation, including the cities of Atlantic City, New Orleans, Charlottesville, and Madison, Wisconsin.

With the growth of his companies, in 1859, this family patriarch purchased a Philadelphia office building for $76,500.[2] This investment made it possible to contain all of the family's business headquarters at the same location of 400 Chestnut Street. Later, the Wood sons retained Quaker architect Addison Hutton to redesign the building into a high-rise to meet the demands of their growing conglomerate.

Richard, Sr.'s death at 70 years came April 1, 1869, at his Philadelphia home of 1121 Arch Street due to respiratory failure. Prior to his death, he had the firm reestablished as R.D. Wood & Sons.

This powerful family's empire would now operate under the direction of the six Woods' sons with their wide range of professional interests and ages ranging from teens to mid thirties. Richard, Edward, Randolph, George, Walter, and Stewart each had a specialty business assignment. Richard, Jr., and Randolph were partners in the mercantile business; Walter and Stewart managed the Florence Iron Works; Richard, Jr., and Edward handled the company's financing while George and his wife, Mary (née Hunn), continued to oversee Millville's operations.

The family's Quaker upbringing was evident in their propensity for benevolent giving. Their Philadelphian community has been the very fortunate recipients of their most charitable donations. The foundations they have supported include the University of Pennsylvania, the Pennsylvania Hospital, the Philadelphia College of Physicians, the Children's Hospital of Philadelphia, the Academy of Natural Sciences, and more.

With their conscientious and conservative business practices, their companies and those that they funded continued to be largely successful. The brothers sat on one another's boards, so management decisions could be made in the best interests of the family. Honoring their father's visions for the future, Richard, Jr., and George developed the WJ&A from Newfield to Atlantic City via a new spur through Mays Landing.

Richard was appointed founder and director, while his brother George was elected president of this growing corporation. Ambition was not in shortage in the Wood family, as evidenced in the 1906 Edition of Philadelphia's Directory of Directors:

Wood, Edward R., 400 Chestnut Street, Philadelphia
  Millville Improvement Co., President, and Director
  South Jersey Land & Transportation Co., President and Director
  Shade Gap Railroad, President and Director
  Philadelphia Board of Trade, Executive Council
  East Broad Top Railroad & Coal Co., Director
  Rockhill Iron & Coal Co., Director

. . .

Wood, George 400 Chestnut Street and 626 Chestnut Street, Philadelphia

R.D. Wood & Co., Iron Founders

Millville Manufacturing Co., Cotton Goods, President and Director

Mays Landing Water Power Co., President and Director

Philadelphia Manufacturers' Mutual Fire Insurance Co., Vice-President and Director

The Philadelphia National Bank, Director

The Mutual Fire, Marine and Inland Insurance Co., Director

The Pennsylvania Railroad Co., Director

West Jersey & Seashore Railroad Co., Director

The Pennsylvania Steel Co., Director

Pennsylvania Steel Co., of New Jersey, Director

East Broad Top Railroad & Coal Co., Director

Rockhill Iron & Coal Co., Director

Wood, Grahame, 626 Chestnut Street, Philadelphia and Boston, Mass.

Kremer & Sturbing, Dry Goods

Millville Manufacturing Co., Cotton Goods, Director

Wood, Richard VI (Jr.) 400 Chestnut Street, Philadelphia

R.D. Wood & Co., Iron Founders

The Provident Life & Trust Co., of Philadelphia, Director

Mays Landing Water Power Co., Director

Philadelphia Board of Trade, Treasurer

Haverford College, Manager

Hospital of the University of Pennsylvania, Manager

Wood, Richard D, Sr., 626 Chestnut Street, Philadelphia

Millville Manufacturing Co., Cotton Goods, Vice-President, Secretary & Director

. . .

Wood, Stuart, 400 Chestnut Street, Philadelphia
R.D. Wood & Co., Iron Founders
Market Street National Bank
Mortgage Trust Company of Pennsylvania, Director
Macon Gas Light & Water Co., Treasurer and Director
Mays Landing Water Power Co., Director

Wood, Walter, 400 Chestnut Street, Philadelphia
R.D. Wood & Co., Iron Founders
Trades League of Philadelphia, Director
Philadelphia Bourse, commodities exchange, Director
National State Bank (Camden), Director
Haverford College, Manager

In the late 1870s, the Wood family prepared for one of their biggest challenges yet: the launch of their city-to-shore rail line. Freight trains would move goods generated by the company's mills, while passenger cars would run round-trip excursions from Philadelphia to Atlantic City. In November 1879, the WJ&A was incorporated. The fleet included:

- six locomotives for $7,500 each, or $196,363 in today's dollars.
- 40 first-class passenger cars, costing $2,000 each, or $48,555 today.

The mortgage, payable in 1896, was for $1 million, would equate to $26,181,764 today.

PENNSYLVANIA RAILROAD ENGINES
CLASS D2 4-4-0 AND CLASS D4 4-4-0,
MANUFACTURED IN ALTOONA, PA.

Two of the new steam locomotive Class D2 4-4-0 and D4 4-4-0 engines, acquired from the PRR in Altoona, Pa., were the largest "Americans" on the railroad. Larger locomotives were used exclusively for the heavy Atlantic City excursion service, being six tons heavier than their predecessor.

D2s burned soft coal, noted for producing more ash in the exhaust. The D4 engines featured a longer firebox to incinerate slower-burning anthracite coal. Called "hard coal," anthracite was considered the highest-ranking coal product for its peak carbon and energy content. In addition, it provided a cleaner burn with the fewest impurities and cinders, equating to safer rails and cleaner trails on South Jersey's pine bristled railways, as well as reducing the chance of forest fires in the Pinelands.

In preparation for the launch of the WJ&A in June 1880, the fleet was completed and readied for operation within the year. Foreseeing a successful future for the Line, in meeting minutes from the PRR dated August 6, 1880, the following entry was made: "a discussion of building a potential year-round hotel in Cape May in cooperation with the WJ&A." A special committee was assigned to review the feasibility of such an investment; however, subsequent meeting minutes did not mention any follow-up by the special committee.

The next order of business for the WJ&A was to assemble the necessary workforce to accomplish their goals for the year; they wouldn't have far to look. Several of the city's ethnic neighborhoods were home to a generation of children of survivors of Ireland's Great Potato Famine of 1845. During that period, 14 million immigrants relocated to the United States, providing companies with an eager and willing workforce. For workers in the Wood's businesses, prospects for the new year already looked promising. By the end of January 1880, teams of men were at work with Mays Landing Construction on the Great Egg Harbor Rivers' trestle bridge.

City by the Sea

Dr. Jonathan Pitney and businessman Richard Summers were hailed as the visionaries behind the creation of a citywide seaside resort. Richard Osborne, an Irish-born civil engineer, designed a grid system to make it easier to navigate the city's streets. With the approval of the railroad board in Philadelphia, he coined the name "Atlantic City" for this 11.92 square mile city-to-be. Avenues would later be named after the world's oceans, intersecting with streets named after America's states — numbered to 27 in the later 19th century. The significance of the railroad to the development of the state's tourism industry cannot be overstated.

In March 1852, New Jersey granted the Camden and Atlantic Railroad Company a charter to build and operate a rail line to Atlantic City, privileged to be the first of its kind. The unveiling would commence on July 4, 1854, welcoming eager travelers from up and down the eastern seaboard. Several hotels opened within two years of the inaugural train, including the Surf House, Congress Hall, and the Mansion House. The final spike on the second city-to-shore railroad, Philadelphia and Atlantic City, was driven in July 1877. By the time WJ&A launched in the summer of 1880, the Boardwalk had already been part of the landscape for 10 years. An estimated 20,000 Philadelphians traveled to Atlantic City each weekend during the high season, adding to the year-round population of 14,000.

ATLANTIC CITY'S FIRST VISITORS CAME BY HORSE-DRAWN CARRIAGES,
WAGONS AND STEAMSHIPS.

The first WJ&A excursion on June 16, 1880, carried both stock-holders and members of the press in four new passenger coaches, where they arrived at the intersection of the beach and Florida Avenue. With fanfare only a few in South Jersey had ever witnessed, the "Queen of Resorts" was born. Atlantic City was quickly becoming America's favorite seaside resort and playground.

One tradition that Atlantic City and the railroads could both claim was the development of the vacation industry. By introducing the "city to the shore" excursion as an affordable luxury, even those with the most modest means could plan on some time away to escape the over-crowded cities. A *New York Times* article in 1883 concluded, "Patrons are all Philadelphians, of the small merchant and artisan class, who cannot afford the time or cash to go further away from home." As the shore became more accessible, both working and middle-class families were more inclined to expect vacation time and compensation. "Summering" was a concept that would become a nationally recognized benefit, thanks to tourism development at the Jersey Shore. During this era of industrial growth, the Westinghouse Air Brake Company also realized the value of providing company benefits to their workforce and their positive impact on productivity. By the late 1800s, they had equipped over two million freight, passenger, mail, baggage, and express cars and 89,000 locomotives with Westinghouse Air Brakes.

ON THE BOARDWALK IN ATLANTIC CITY

Alexander Boardman, a railroad conductor, and hotelier Jacob Keim had presented the city with the idea of constructing an exterior wooden walk. To quell the incessant battle with nature, they conceived an idea to minimize the accumulation of sand in railroad cars and carpeted hotel lobbies. With the council's approval, tax revenues were used to build an eight-foot-wide temporary wooden structure that could be dismantled and stored during the off-season. Later, city management officially named the wooden walkway the "Boardwalk," and promoted it as a symbol of the city since 1870. A decade later, a second Boardwalk, fourteen feet in width, replaced the first, extending from the Absecon Lighthouse to the Seaview Excursion House. An attraction in its own right, one side overlooked an impressive span of ocean coastline. At the same time, the other offered a view of the most luxuriously appointed hotels of the day. It continues to be a preferred alternative for comfortable walking and maintenance-free sand control.

THE UNITED STATES HOTEL, ATLANTIC CITY.

The United States Hotel had the distinction of being both the first public hotel in Atlantic City and the largest in the nation. In its early years, the hotel provided housing for construction and railroad teams, reporters, and investors who worked together, building the city's infrastructure.

Later, the four-story hotel would have up to 600 rooms to accommodate more than 2,000 guests. Its most celebrated guest was the 18th U.S. President, Ulysses S. Grant, in 1874, introducing a new era of clientele to the city.

Other grand hotel properties featuring modern amenities included the Dennis, now part of Bally's Park Place Casino Hotel, and the Chalfonte and Haddon Hall, now part of Resorts Casino Hotel. Mule-powered streetcars became a popular form of transportation on city avenues during this period of rapid development. By the turn of the century, Atlantic City had become a world-renowned resort.

In South Atlantic City, later known as Margate, real estate speculator James Lafferty of Philadelphia, was at work commissioning a most unusual oddity. Within the year, construction would be completed on a six-story elephant-shaped building, the first of three but the last one still standing. When it opened in 1881, tourists flocked from Atlantic City by rail and from Ocean City by steamboat.

Originally known as the Elephant Bazaar, she would come to be known as "Lucy, the Margate Elephant." More than a century later, Lucy continues her watch over the Margate beaches while standing tall through seasons of North Atlantic storms. She carries the recognition of being the "Oldest Roadside Attraction in the United States."

Back up at the north beach, a first ocean pier extending from the Boardwalk was under construction. Built with steel and concrete, the first was scheduled for completion in 1882.

As the building boom continued, five similar piers would be built within a decade exclusively for seaside recreation. Offerings included amusements, games, rides, exhibits, and entertainment. Soon after, they would expand to offer swimming pools, bowling alleys, shuffleboard, animal shows, celebrities, comedians, singers, and big bands.

Another Boardwalk tradition was introduced in 1876. The Atlantic City Easter Parade would become an annual event, attracting as many as 100,000 visitors, strolling the Boardwalk in their Sunday best. The intent was to capture a percentage of the same-sized crowds who attended the 1876 Centennial Exposition, hosted in Philadelphia. The 100th anniversary of America's independence was the first official World's Fair in the United States, attracting nearly 10 million visitors.

A treat that first became popular on the Boardwalk has had a special appeal among many younger travelers — a sampling from one, or several, of the 18 confectioners offering a popular new candy created by David Bradley. Boardwalk sweet shops called it 'saltwater taffy.' In no time, it would become Atlantic City's favorite take-home souvenir, a timeless treat made by one of the seashore's first retailers. The memories it invokes of the oceans' salty sea air along with its' ability to withstand the summer's heat and humidity, has made saltwater taffy one of the most popular remembrances of a seashore vacation.

PLANNING THE EXCURSION

Like inland metropolitan dwellers today, 19th century east coast inhabitants were eager to experience a summer day trip at the seashore to escape the extreme August temperatures. The Literary Society of St. Anne's Catholic Church of northwest Philadelphia would be the first and largest summer excursion to Atlantic City that year. Founded in 1845 on Lehigh Avenue and Memphis Streets, St. Anne's is an Irish Catholic parish community in the Archdiocese of Philadelphia, still serving Kensington, Fishtown, and Port Richmond.

ST. ANNE'S ROMAN CATHOLIC CHURCH.

In addition to his congregation, the pastor of St. Anne's, Rev. Thomas Kieran, extended invitations to join the pleasure trip to the neighboring parishes of St. Michael's, Church of Annunciation, and Church of the Immaculate Conception, as well as Church of the Messiah and the Third Street Methodist Episcopal Church in Camden. Philadelphia's working class would be well represented on their earned trip to the Jersey coast. Several registered travelers were Irish Catholic girls who had come to America ahead of their families to establish a second chance for a good life in America. Recognized as the center of social activity among church parishioners, St. Anne's Literary Society was considered a haven for Irish Catholics newly arrived in Philadelphia. Their members welcomed a day to wander beyond the city's limits and explore the ocean seacoast while raising funds for their church. Reverend Francis J. Quinn, assistant pastor, and

Thomas P. Judge, president of the Literary Institute and their committee, coordinated the 15-hour excursion at a modest group fare:

- For parties of 1000+, $.60 excursion fare roundtrip, or $15.71 per ticket today.
- Transient fares for adults round trip $1.00 or $26.18 apiece today.
- Children's fares $.50 roundtrip or $13.09 each now.

The first leg of the excursion would take the group from their River Ward neighborhoods of Philadelphia to the wharves at Market Street to board the ferries.

❦ 2 ❧

A LL ABOARD!
AUGUST 11, 1880

Gulls overhead fished for their morning meal as the sun broke over the horizon. The stench of decaying sea life combined with disintegrating trash overwhelmed the wharves along the Delaware River. Just another August day on Philadelphia's shoreline.

The early Wednesday weather condition appeared overcast and breezy for the sunrise ferry crossing as the eager travelers began arriving for their 6:15 a.m. departure at the Market Street terminal. Their journey began with hordes of passengers boarding the six idling water transports. Standing among them were the waged commuters of the more than 150 Camden factories, bound for the West Jersey Ferry Terminal. As this was a private charter for St. Anne's, additional ferries were brought in to service the additional foot traffic on their upper decks.

MARKET STREET FERRY, PHILADELPHIA.

West Jersey's own 'city to shore' excursion was in operation just under eight weeks on August 11, 1880. Upwards of 1,300 travelers from St. Anne's and the neighboring parishes had reservations to travel together under the power of one train to Atlantic City. Contrary to initial arrangements with the committee, the PRR determined that the group would be divided into two sections of railroad cars, the lead 16-car consist followed by the second, an eight-car consist.

With hundreds of excursionists arriving for the 7:15 a.m. train to Atlantic City, a change in the alignment would have delayed the departure time. The committee members voiced their dissatisfaction with the change in plans to the station management, but they proceeded with the new arrangements. Despite the revision, passengers boarded the trains giddy with excitement. Once settled, they tucked their shoebox lunches safely away under their seats and prepared for the day's adventures. In time, Philadelphian travelers going 'down the shore' would come to be referred to as "Shoobies" as a scurrilous reference to their shoebox lunches.

As the temperatures increased with the daylight hours, so too did the morning chatter amongst the passengers. In the last seat, in the last car of the first train, Louis Moore sat alone. Smartly dressed, he lit his pipe and squinted his eyes, scanning the morning newspaper head-lines. His tobacco created a noxious cloud that enveloped the last rows of the train car and mixed with the stale scent from the prior indul-gence of another passenger.

On the opposite bench, dressed in ragged blue overalls and a shirt stained from perspiration, sat 40-year-old Thomas McGrath. His unshaven face and grungy dress suggested an appearance of an old railroad man in need of some bay rum to mask his obvious "summer-time fragrance." A nagging, persistent cough flared up as the smoke cloud reached his corner of the train car. He clumsily produced a stained handkerchief from his front pocket to reveal a piece of hard soda bread intended as his rations for the day. He kept the hanky out, as needed for his cough and took two small bites of the stale bread before tucking the remaining piece back into his overall's front pocket, followed by another coughing spell. As a sufferer of Consumption, he was unable to work in the rail yards any longer, with symptoms of a bloodied hacking cough, fatigue, and debilitating pain in his lungs. His widowed neighbor, Mrs. McSorley, who lived in the tenement above, would make him a loaf of Irish soda bread every Saturday along with at least a bowl or two of Irish stew. This being Wednesday, the remnant soda bread left had already lost its fresh-ness. Being sensitive to his situation, Mrs. McSorley was aware that he was without the means to provide for himself. She had won an excursion ticket in a raffle for her church's Literacy Society and gave it to him in the hope that the fresh ocean air would help relieve his discomfort some. While sitting across the aisle from Mr. Louis Moore for nearly two hours, he hoped that the pipe smoke would not kill him first.

Sitting in the passenger car in front of both men were their Irish friends, neighbors and fellow parish members:

David and Margarette McCrystal bounced their 4-month-old, Catherine, and 20-month-old, Margaret, on their laps. With them was their 11-year-old nurse and niece, Katie Walsh, who was absorbed in Louisa May Alcott's novel, *Little Women*.

Sitting directly in front of the McCrystal family were 16-year-old Lavinia Grace and her mother Elizabeth. They looked forward to her sister's upcoming nuptials, just days away. Both were preoccupied with preparations for the wedding as they completed the finishing touches on their Irish lace needlework.

Older sister (and bride-to-be), Lillie Grace, sat ahead of her mother and sister with her fiancé, John Devlin, and another couple, Mary Hanratty and Henry Bender. Henry's brother, James Bender, also came along and brought his friend, James Sweeney, and his brother, Alexander, for the day. The gentlemen were eager to jump into the ocean's surf, and the ladies were perfectly content with being spectators for that event.

Sitting alone was a seemingly independent 12-year-old, Joseph McGovern. His unkempt presentation gave the impression of a lack of adult supervision at home.

Ahead of the men in the last row was 4-year-old Freddy Carr, sitting with his parents and his aunt and uncle, who had given him with a "cup and ball" game for his first trip to the shore. The Carr Family were neighbors of Mr. McGrath and Mrs. McSorley, who lived next door.

Seated in front of them were sisters Rose and Kate Murphy, 19- and 22-years-old, respectively, who were happy just to be spending the day together. They both missed their parents, who were still in their beloved homeland.

Sisters Ellen and Kate Shields brought along a friend, 12-year-old Anne Gillespie, who kept busy recording the day's events in her diary. Anne also brought along her *Oliver Twist* novel, hoping there would be time during the day to read on the beach. There was already someone who reminded her of the Dickens character "come to life," an untidy boy sitting by himself two rows behind her.

Sarah Wright, 19, and her mother Emma, 35, celebrated a special mother and daughter day out together. Mr. Wright, unfortunately, was unable to get the day off from his job piloting the ferries to join them. They sat in front of the Shields sisters.

Friends Owen Walsh, Patrick McBride, and Henry McCann went a couple of rows ahead, setting up a friendly game of checkers against their rivals, the Sweeney brothers.

Opposite them sat a young married couple, Bill and Mary Ann Gallagher, on their first day away together since their wedding the prior month. Mary Ann's parents had not approved of their daughter's choice in a husband, and after not attending the ceremony, sadly, they still were not speaking to her.

In the front row, furthest away, were two little "red-headed doll babies," Mary and Annie Kelly seated alongside their mother. These Irish twins had a soda cracker for breakfast in each one of their little hands while they sang their rendition of "Polly Wolly Doodle All Day" to the delight of their surrounding passengers.

Scattered about the car were pairs of teen girls. Each one was very eager to arrive "Down the Shore" and hopefully return with a potential husband at the end of the day.

Many of the travelers amongst the thirteen hundred were quite content just watching the changing scenery out the trains' passenger windows. In no time, they were crossing Cooper Creek on a single track bound for the New Jersey Shore.

Just after departing the city, the landscape changed drastically to a dense forest with intermittent sunlight streaming through the pine and oak trees. "We must be in the wilderness, folks," young Joseph McGovern remarked as he looked around to see if anyone was paying attention to his comment. He cupped his hands around his mouth, pretending to make an announcement. "We've entered the New Jersey Pine Barrens, ladies and gentlemen; one hundred thousand welcomes," he said, quoting an old Irish saying. The groups of passengers nearby were too engaged in their conversations to respond. Recognizing that no one was listening, Joseph returned his gaze to the abundant forest beyond the railbed. "Well, I bet Tom Sawyer would have enjoyed this adventure in the wilderness," he mumbled under his breath. He took out the pocket knife that his father had given him and sliced himself an apple as a morning snack. Anne Gillespie turned her head away from her diary for a moment, noticing that young Joseph appeared to be having a conversation with himself. "He must be very lonely," she thought. The 12-year-old then went back to writing in her diary.

Sarah Collins and Mary Green had been friends since grammar school. They took Irish dance classes together, attended the same Catholic school classes, and were hired together at Dolan's Cotton Mill on the same day. On Sundays, they attended 8 a.m. mass at St. Anne's together. Neither of them had been "lucky in love" with their 11-hour workdays on their six-day workweeks. Their schedules made it difficult to socialize with so much to catch up on at home in one day. They had been waiting for this trip to Atlantic City since February when Archbishop Wood's office first announced it. They were hopeful that after waiting six months, their 'luck' was about to change.

Seated a row ahead of them were Charles Frost and his brother, William, who couldn't help but notice that there were "more than a few" lasses on this excursion. With business at their Irish pub doing well, the brothers were ready to start settling down. When Mary Green's train ticket fell under the bench where they were seated, it seemed like the perfect time to make an introduction. Ideally, for Mary and Sarah, both men were in their late 20s and single — but looking to settle down.

The brothers spoke proudly of their hand-carved bar, hearty menu, Irish storytellers, and traditional Irish music that had made their pub a favorite among the locals in the neighborhood. The four travelers would continue their conversation throughout the rest of the day. The young friends hoped to meet potential suitors, and the brothers hoped to meet potential wives. Might this just be their "Luck of the Irish?"

As the trains traveled deeper into the Pines, they came upon a small village, somewhere between the city and the shore. The conductor was quick to mention that they were passing through "Mays Landing" and they would be reaching their destination of Atlantic City within the hour.

Nearby two couples sat beside one another. They were neighbors and friends, and both were engaged to be married within the month. Mary Hanratty and Henry Bender were weeks away from their nuptials, while Lillie Grace and John Devlin were just days away from theirs. They all welcomed a day away from wedding planning in exchange for the company of good friends, a picnic lunch, and an inviting seashore.

"Thank you, conductor," replied one of the ladies.

"I don't imagine we'll ever be visiting Mays Landing, but at least we can say we passed through it," remarked John.

His fiancé Lillie reminded him, "Someday when we find the 'streets that were lined with gold,' we may buy a one-way ticket back!"

"Well, enjoy yourselves at the seashore today," the conductor replied, "and remember, some gifts are worth waiting for, like the gift of a rainbow at the end of a storm." The rainbow sounded more probable on an overcast day than streets lined with gold.

As the trains approached the bays, the terrain changed dramatically once again, transitioning from a dense forest to a wet tidal marsh called "the meadows." The aroma of decomposing vegetation was a sure sign that they were nearing their destination. Moments later, as the excursion was on their final approach, the locomotives began tolling their engine bells to announce their arrival in Absecon at 9 a.m. A rail bridge to Atlantic City would not be completed until 1885, so the group disembarked and continued onto the wharf to be ferried across the channel. After a short transfer to Absecon Island, the eager excursionists left the platform and hurried up to the famous Boardwalk to get their first glimpse of the beautiful "city by the sea."

"Don't forget your shoebox lunches," the conductor reminded everyone.

The first moments for the anxious travelers commenced with their collective admiration for the natural beaches, dune grasses, and refreshing ocean breezes. Overhead, squawking gulls mixed with the sounds of waves pummeling the shoreline. After having experienced the foulness of the salt marshes, they inhaled the freshness of the ocean's air. Younger children, including Freddy Carr and the Kelly sisters, immediately began exploring the beach and collecting seashells as their contented parents smiled, admiring the refreshing change of scenery. Others looked out over the mighty Atlantic Ocean and became visibly emotional. For some, loved ones still waited on the other side of the vastness for a fresh start in America. On this side of the Atlantic, many here were still waiting too. Rose and Kate Murphy had left their homeland two years before and worked at the mill to reunite their family in Philadelphia.

"Christmas," whispered Kate. "My goal is to have them here for Christmas."

"Well, we'd better get started practicing some Christmas carols then." Rose smiled as her eyes welled up with happy tears.

A gaggle of ladies opened their stylish parasols to shade the mid-morning sun as their Victorian updos fluttered amidst the shore's summer breezes. Perfect weather for strolling along the seacoast in their modest attire to "people watch" the latest in (beach-inspired) fashions. Sarah Wright and her mother Emma had heard that the Beach House rented "beach costumes" for 25 cents and decided to indulge in some "beach bathing decorum." From the Boardwalk, a party of ladies from the excursion observed with curious interest that Sarah and Emma had changed into black, knee-length wool flannel dresses, accentuated with sailor collars, worn over bloomers, and trimmed in ribbons and bows. Stockings with canvas shoes completed their "unique" bathing ensembles. Their 25 cent fee included a portable changing room dragged into the sea by an attendant to enter and exit the surf. These private "bathing machines" resembled closets on wooden carts for the sea-modest Victorians. "A shame your father had to work today and is missing all of this fine entertainment," joked Emma to her daughter as they frolicked in the surf. William Wright was employed by the Camden and Philadelphia Ferry Company. He hoped that the three of them could return to the shore before the season ended on Labor Day, just three and a half weeks away.

A "BATHING MACHINE" IN THE SURF.

Meanwhile, a group of young men from their excursion raced up the beach, looking for the biggest waves to chase. Life in the big city of Philadelphia was certainly different from life at New Jersey's seashore.

Some of the travelers wandered along the Boardwalk to Pacific Avenue and down to the towering Absecon Lighthouse. The Irish visitors were surprised to learn that this landmark was designed and built by a fellow Irishman and native of Philadelphia, George Meade, later the Commanding Officer of Union Forces in the Civil War. Major General Meade is best known for defeating Confederate General Robert E. Lee at the Battle of Gettysburg six years after building this lighthouse. Meade's great-grandfather, Robert Meade, came from Ireland and settled in Philadelphia, becoming an active supporter of the Catholic Church there. General Meade now rests in Laurel Hill Cemetery in Philadelphia. Several in the group recognized the name Gettysburg, in which their family and neighbors had also fought. Philadelphia's Irish Brigade of Pennsylvania's 69th had played a key role during the battle, helping to turn the tide of the Civil War with a Northern victory.

For one of the few times that morning, Joseph McGovern raised his voice, "My grandfather carried the green Irish flag at Pickett's Charge with General Meade." He followed with: "He now rests with my father and 37 other veterans of the Brigade in St. Anne's churchyard. A proud Irish soldier he was." Joseph spoke like a proud and lonely Irishman himself.

ABSECON LIGHTHOUSE IN ATLANTIC CITY.

As the group departed the lighthouse, hungry gulls sailed above, hoping that crumbs of any kind were among the discarded shoe boxes. Luck wasn't with the "winged scavengers" that day. Ladies tied down their hats as the wind picked up and checked their wristwatches as the men pulled out their pocket watches from their trousers to see how much time they had left. "Half-past four o'clock," announced James Sweeney. "We still have an hour before we have to be back at the station. Hopefully the rain will hold off." That came as welcomed news to the two 12-year-olds, Anne Gillespie and Joseph McGovern. They had just passed a set of swings that they were eager to try out. Now, with the extra time, they could still add it into their day's "adventure list."

Sarah Collins and Mary Green had a lovely afternoon with their escorts, Charles and William Frost. They playfully nicknamed them the "Pub Brothers" as the four travelers seemed quite smitten with their new friendships.

"Charles makes a mighty good Shepard's Pie. Would you ladies care to join us at the Pub for dinner tomorrow night?" asked William.

"That sounds like a perfectly wonderful way to end the day. We accept and thank you for the invitation," Mary replied for both herself and Sarah with a girlish grin. The two couples gingerly strolled back, hand in hand, to the Excursion House.

AN "EXCURSION DAY" IN ATLANTIC CITY.

Ellen Shields, 24, had offered to chaperone Anne Gillespie on the excursion. Anne's parents allowed her to go, but not without her father's concerns. Ellen had assured him that his daughter would be in responsible hands. Of course, that was before Anne had asked to join Joseph on the beach swings.

"He looks like he could really use a friend. I think he's lonely," she said to both Ellen and Kate. "May I? Just for 20 minutes." There was no denying her heart was in the right place.

Ellen could see no harm in showing some compassion to someone who was a lonely soul. "Go along," she said. "We'll be waiting for you right here."

Joining them on the benches to rest their weary feet were 4-year-old Freddy Carr, his parents, aunt, and uncle.

Ellen had seen Julia Carr at church before. "Did this big boy have a good time today?" she asked his mother.

"I think we all did. Just maybe missed that afternoon nap, but I'm sure once the train starts moving, he'll be in 'La La Land,'" said his mother.

Seated behind them on another park bench was William and Mary Ann Gallagher, from the neighborhood. They had just been married five weeks. Watching little Freddy, Mrs. Gallagher smiled and said wistfully, "We're hoping for a 'little Freddy' of our own someday."

Everyone sitting nearby congratulated the young couple on the nuptials. Mrs. Carr said, "I hope any child you have will be as much of a blessing as this one has been to us," smiling at her young son. "We've been blessed with such a good boy." Freddy, realizing that he was the "good boy" to whom his mother was referring, gave them the biggest big boy smile his little face could muster.

Thomas McGrath, their neighbor, sat beside them in obvious respiratory distress. Breathing deeply, he slowly regained his composure and assured everyone that he just needed to rest.

The older boys, wanting to challenge each other again, decided to race along the beach for 45 minutes, a track they had never seen in the city. From somewhere in the group was heard: "Be prepared, Sweeneys. We're going to slaughter you in the checkers rematch." The older girls decided to strike out on their own and find a more appealing source of entertainment.

The two brides-to-be, Lillie Grace and Mary Hanratty, exchanged notes on Irish wedding customs while they waited to return to the Excursion House. Realizing how close it was to their wedding days, they were glad to know a fellow Irish bride with whom to review the details. They checked off the following:

The Claddagh ring: representing the three beacons of successful marriage; friendship in the shape of hands; loyalty as the symbol of the crown; and love by the heart. Traditionally presented by an Irish mother of the bride to her daughter.

"The tying of the knot:" a ceremonial tradition of wrapping the couple's hands in fabric and knotting their hands together. The love knot representing unity through thick and thin.

White Irish lace: included somewhere in the bride's trousseau; fabric of the wedding dress, a hanky, or stationary. The lace signified resilience after tragedy.

"I think I'm ready to get married now," joked Lillie.

"I'm available Saturday – as long as it doesn't rain," her soon-to-be husband, John, joked back. The two couples stood before the ocean, praying for beautiful weather on their wedding days — without a cloud in the skies.

"I've got the Irish lace covered," chimed in Lillie's younger sister, Lavinia. Their mother, Elizabeth, smiled as she redirected her younger daughter to the station house.

A group of teen girls who sat near each other on the train car now sat together on the beach, writing messages in the sand. "I have a bit of a foolhardy suggestion," offered one of the Murphy sisters. "We could sing some Christmas carols that everyone knows." The group laughed at the notion of singing "Deck the Halls" in August but participated in the sing-along. And Rose was right; everyone did know all of the words. "This one's for you, Mum and Daddy," Rose Murphy whispered as she winked and shared a smile with her sister Kate.

The McCrystal Family sat together nearby on their blanket, listening to their season favorites, while embracing their two young daughters and their niece, Katie Walsh, in a big family hug. Katie had learned a lot about Christmas traditions and decorating with greens and holly from reading *Little Women*. Coincidentally, they had passed thousands of holly trees in the Pine Barrens on their morning train ride.

"I learned a new 'tree trick' today since we seem to be celebrating Christmas in August! Did you know if you grow four holly trees together that you'll get red Christmas berries?" Katie asked. It made her aunt and uncle proud just to witness Katie's excitement and her appreciation for nature's abundant gifts. "This has been such a special day," she said. "I love when we can spend family time like this, especially outdoors!"

"I wish I could just wrap this day up and hold onto it forever," she said, as she took in a deep breath of the ocean's fresh air.

David and Margarette agreed Katie had become very nurturing toward her two little cousins. She was constantly reading to them and sharing sisterly affections. Privately, David suggested, "We should plan on getting Clement Moore's book, *A Visit from St. Nicholas* for her to read to the girls."

"At the rate she is going, by Christmas, she'll be reading them Scrooge and Marley's Ghost," his wife joked back.

"You know, on the train this morning, there was a girl about Katie's age who was reading a Charles Dickens' novel, *Oliver Twist*, I think," said David.

"Oh... that's... Anne... Gillespie, she is just a year, she is just a year old...older." Without a warning, Margarette's breathing became labored, followed by a sort of minor paralysis. Her young family watched helplessly while she struggled for each breath. "I feel like my insides are burning up," she said, as she tried to wave her handkerchief.

Then as quickly as the sensation came, in an instant, it was gone. She later confided to David that she couldn't explain it, but she feared for their family's safety. Her intuition was telling her to pray for protection.

"Race you!" Anne shouted. Joseph ran ahead of her and grabbed the swing closest to the end first. His first victory for the day, but his win lost in his absence of gentility. They both tried to reach the highest point before the other, each exerting their best efforts. Once they had reached a comfortable height, the motion and the conversation flowed easily.

As they swung, Joseph shared that he had been sent to an orphanage in New York but managed to escape in a freight car and ferry back to Philadelphia. He had only just arrived this week and knew to go directly to his former parish for sanctuary. Father Kieran provided him some gruel and helped young Joseph find work.

"I'm going to be a newsboy with the city paper," said Joseph, then tried out his announcing skills. "Papers, Get your Papers Here!"

Joseph looked over at Anne. "Father Kieran arranged that I will start selling papers Friday morning at six o'clock. I'll work as late as I have to make back the 50 cents for 100 papers that I have to put out upfront. Plus, I make 20 cents a day."

Anne had been reading a tale by Charles Dickens about an orphan boy and his urchin friends who also lived in an orphanage, ate gruel, and spent long hours at the workhouse.

"Your story is starting to sound a lot like *Oliver Twist*. You should read my book so you don't end up falling into favor with the likes of the same kind of unsavory characters, unless *I* can be your 'Artful Dodger!'" said Anne with a 'cockney' accent. With that, she took the lead on the swing. "My Papa says, 'poetry, art, and music make for a peaceful soul,' but I prefer a good 'Dickensian' novel."

"Your papa sounds like a smart man," said Joseph, jumping off of his swing. "My mother had a way with words, too. She would tell me, 'those we love are never really gone. They're just a whisper in the wind,'" he said, saving his tears for another day. Changing the subject, he asked, "Do you think I could borrow your *Oliver Twist*, sometime?"

"Of course," replied Anne, as she jumped from her swing. "Here you go." Pulling the book out from her pile of belongings, she handed him one of her priceless treasures. "When you're finished with that one, I have *A Christmas Carol*. That's a good one as well. At least you'll have something to read on the train ride home tonight, before you start your 'newsie' job."

"Thank you, 'Artful Dodger,'" said a grateful "Oliver" McGovern.

Seeing the two had finished with their swinging, Ellen Shields motioned to Anne to join her and sister Kate Shields, as the whipping wind had slowed to an eerie quietness. Ominous storm clouds gathered overhead while the angry Atlantic Ocean prepared for a showdown.

"I'll be right there," Anne yelled into the wind.

For a moment, Joseph appeared distracted, picking up a stick to sharpen with his pocket knife, the last thing his father had given him before tuberculosis left him an orphan. "Just one more thing before we leave for the station house," he said.

Dragging the stick through the packed sand, he appeared to be spelling something out. "How do you spell your name?" he asked a minute later.

"A-N-N-E," she said. Concerned about the approaching storm, she tried to hasten things along by peering over his shoulder to see what he was concocting. He finished quickly enough to step aside so she could read the message. The first line was the date: "August 11, 1880." The second line read: "THE. SHOOBIES. WERE. HERE. Joseph and Anne."

Anne giggled at his quick wit. "Now there's an entry for my diary!" said the budding journalist.

They ran to join Ellen and Kate; then the four tried to outrun the rain. As luck would have it, that was precisely when the skies opened up.

The rest of the 1,300 travelers were making their way back to the West Jersey Excursion House for their return trip when the summer humidity triggered the anticipated storm. Hail, the size of marbles, came raining down on those still waiting to board. Despite the deteriorating weather condition, even with the mix of hail and rain, the darkening clouds didn't appear to dampen the passengers' spirits. Actual post reports for the Atlantic City area later recorded rain after 3 p.m. with intermittent lightning strikes.

Both trains were made ready for the 6:00 p.m. departure back to Philadelphia. Passengers shook off the rainwater and settled down into the car's wooden bench seats. The last call for "All Aboard" went out as the conductor from each section inspected and secured the windows against the ensuing downpour. Passenger Henry McCann refused to have his window closed by the conductor, despite the worsening conditions.

The bells on each of the locomotives' engines began to peel, signaling the train's preparation for departure from the station at New York and Atlantic Avenues. Locomotive No. 262, the lead consist of the two sections, left the platform with Engineer Daniel Cassidy and Conductor Elmer Mayhew in command. According to recorded accounts, No. 262 exited the station at 6:00 p.m. Moments later, at 6:05 p.m., No. 627 followed. Departure orders were given by the station superintendent and later confirmed by Edward Aiken, engineer of the smaller of the two trains. Running slower across the Atlantic City meadows, Engineer Aiken estimated their lag distance at Pleasantville to be approximately eight to nine minutes or two miles behind the lead train.

They continued at a five-minute interval, traveling at a steady clip of 25 miles per hour. Finally, Aiken cut off the steam to the engine with approximately a mile between the first and second train. Outside, thunder clouds rumbled, and lightning bolts crackled as the pelting rain continued under the threatening summer sky. A brief stop, called a "meet," was scheduled 17 miles up at Mays Landing to allow the down express from Camden to pass on the track. While the rainwater leaking into the wooden cars started to form puddles, passengers chatted and occasionally shivered, sharing stories of their day as the train rattled along the steel tracks. Parents held their young children close, trying to warm the littlest hands from the chill of their wet garments, while the older girls amused themselves by singing campfire songs.

As a soaked Anne took to her diary to record the day's adventures, Joseph and Kate Walsh were both lost in the pages of their respective books. James Sweeney had tired of the checker game he and his friends had been placing bets on, particularly since the outcome hadn't been working in his favor.

"I'm going to get some fresh air," he announced as he headed to the exterior platform at the rear of the passenger car. Conductor Mayhew came out within minutes to punch his boarding pass.

"Well, Conductor, I guess that winds down your day," Sweeney remarked.

"Yes, sir, I won't be bothering you anymore," he promised.

Then immersing himself with nature's abundant rain-soaked pine forest and the imagery of a Currier and Ives train reproduction, James inhaled the warm humidity of the summer night. He watched above as the dark ash trail billowed from the engine's smokestack against the backdrop of the evening storm clouds. For a brief moment in time, all was right in the world. He would remain on the rear platform until the trains arrived in Mays Landing.

Inside, several ladies rested their heads on the shoulders of their male companions while children laid their sleepy heads in the gentle cradle of their mothers' cozy laps. Softly, some of the girls continued singing, now Christmas carols, lifting their voices in song like a choir against the rattle of the passenger cars on the wet railroad.

"Silent Night, Holy Night,
All is calm. All is bright.
Round yon Virgin,
Mother and Child
Holy infant so tender and mild
Sleep in heavenly peace."

Father Quinn was quoted later to say, "Every person was very happy and delighted with the manner in which the day had been spent"...

Earlier that day, in a moment of heavenly peace, Katie Walsh wanted to "just wrap this day up and hold onto it forever," spoken like an angel, beyond her eleven years.

꧁ 3 ꧂

On the approach to Mays Landing, No. 627 was now running at approximately 25 miles per hour with 5 miles distance between sections. Engineer Aiken prepared for the wet rails by testing and applying the air brakes a mile and a half prior to the stop. With less than a mile to go, he foresaw a disaster quickly developing on the single track ahead of them at the cut.

At 200 yards, he could see the last car of the 16 in the first train was dead ahead on the bridge over the Great Egg Harbor River and assumed that it was waiting for the switch to be shifted.

Twenty-four passenger cars, two locomotives, and two tenders had to merge onto 2,600 feet[1] of siding in preparation for the down express coming from the opposite direction. The siding extended past the depot over Mill Street and to a smaller bridge on Baker's Swamp.[2] As the second consist neared the approach of the trestle bridge, the panicked engineer blew the whistle four times to warn of the impending impact. Finally, with just seconds to spare at 25 yards, a desperate Aiken threw the engine into reverse. Although traveling at a speed of just 8 miles per hour, there still was not sufficient time nor adequate space to avoid a rear-end collision over the river. In a final attempt to bring the train to a stop, Sam Flower, the fireman, applied the hand brakes. At 10 feet away, Engineer Aiken exclaimed, "Jump for

God's sake, Sam!" as both he and Conductor Hoagland leapt for their lives into the cool, murky water below.

The infamous moment was 6:41 p.m. The sounds of screeching wheels, hissing steam, and steel-on-steel impact were compounded by the screams of passengers being thrown from their seats as the two trains collided over the river. In an instant, the second locomotive plowed a furrow through the last coach, splintering its rear platform to pieces and crushing the wooden passenger car. When the second engine finally came to rest, the roof of the last car of the first train had been lifted over the second locomotive.

Rev. Francis Quinn swiftly jumped from his seat in the last car of the second consist and rushed from one car to the next, trying to quell the commotion among the parishioners. However, it was not until he was escorted to the horrific scene in the front section of the train and the back platform of the first consist that the priest realized the severity of the tragedy.

Before him, at the site of the mishap, was the young James Sweeney. Father Quinn found that Sweeney had sustained a fatal crushing blow to both his skull and his torso as a result of being pinned between the rear platform on which he had been standing and the second engine's front plate, the cowcatcher.

His brother, Alexander, looked about the exterior of his car to find that all of their friends and fellow passengers were trapped inside what could only be compared to the "bowels of hell." A dense cloud of high-pressure steam and bubbling water gushed into the doomed car from the steam engine, choking the air and trapping its victims.

The steam from the ruptured boiler had blown the door wide open while the closed windows, intended to protect the victims against nature's fury, sealed the fate for many children, women and men.

Father Quinn is said to have heard James Sweeney's confession and administered the last rites of the Catholic Church. Alexander had turned away from the scene of the collision, just in time to bear witness to his brother's last moments. Tragically, the older Sweeney succumbed to his injuries in the arms of his distraught parish priest minutes after arriving at Mays Landing. James would be the first victim to lose his life that night, but he would not be the last. His devastated younger brother, although injured himself, dropped to his knees beside

Father Quinn on the rear platform. Drowning in heaven's tears as they fell from the sky, Alexander wailed in overwhelming despair.

Had the damage stopped with the collision, the loss of life might not have been as staggering. After an event equivalent to a pressure cooker explosion, some of the scalded passengers remained seated in a state of shock, unable to move or speak. Such victims included Margarette McCrystal and her infant, Catherine, as well as her niece, Katie.

The engine's cylinder heads were forced open as the headlight, smokestack, and pilot hung from the locomotive's exterior. Despite the damage, Engine No. 627 remained on the trestle, while the tender, carrying the engine's fuel, had uncoupled and derailed. The engineer climbed up on the engine in a desperate effort to extinguish the fire in the boiler.

The first help from the people of Mays Landing came just moments after the collision. Most households had a member employed at the cotton mill who had just arrived home from the day's work. Families were sitting down to dinner that stormy night when the horrific sound of the two trains colliding over the river broke the steady rhythm of the pelting rain.

The men of the town came running from all directions, while their wives were putting on pots of fresh coffee to deliver to the crash site. No one was prepared for the enormity of what they were about to confront.

This day's excursion was, by far, the biggest of WJ&A's inaugural season. Looking down the tracks, passenger cars lined the railroad as far as the eye could see. As the hundreds of travelers began to leave their respective cars to survey the damage, the severity of the disaster began to be revealed. More than 100 people needed medical attention; The closest hospital was 50 miles away in Philadelphia. Many people needed to be rescued from the Great Egg Harbor River. Upwards of 1,300 passengers were stranded without basic necessities, having only the resources this small community could offer. Whatever this town had, its residents were prepared to share.

No one person or persons were specifically organizing the rescue effort. Villagers just came to pitch in wherever they saw a need. The men of Mays Landing worked together as a team to free victims from the passenger car and rescue those struggling in the tidal river. In the meantime, the women of the community worked diligently to formulate a plan of care for their stranded guests. Nearly everyone agreed to take on a family, or two, perhaps three at their residences. There they would share what rations they had, not knowing how or when help would arrive. As news of the tragedy reached neighboring towns, residents began arriving with food, blankets, and medical supplies. The injured were moved to hotels and taverns about the village, where they could be collectively cared for. One scenario they hadn't considered was what to do with the dead.

Passenger Louis Moore, upon being interviewed later by *The Philadelphia Press*, remarked that he had been seated reading a newspaper and enjoying his pipe on the approach to Mays Landing when he noticed that the section behind them was traveling at a high rate of speed.

Upon seeing several people leaping from the first car, he realized there would be no escaping a collision, so he, too, jumped down the right side of the embankment onto the slimy marsh. Moore ran from the tracks as the second locomotive bulldozed its way into a third of the car where he had just been sitting.

Witnesses found a young man blinded by the scorching steam. Being alone and unknowing which direction to turn to escape, the boy plunged his head through what he thought was an opened window, severely cutting his face and neck by the shards of broken glass. It was later reported that young Joseph McGovern had not survived his injuries.

Others followed suit by breaking windows to hurl themselves and their children into the Great Egg Harbor River below. Ending up in waist-deep water and swampy conditions, they sought relief from their excruciating burns as a different enemy attacked their open wounds with infection. More victims broke through the glass in a state of panic, desperately trying to outrun the scalding steam. Among them was a father, David McCrystal, who intentionally dropped his 20-month-old daughter, Margaret, out of a broken window into the river below. He jumped into the water behind her, but he could not outrun the nemesis that had declared "war" on his family. After their unimaginable suffering, David would lose his wife, Margarette, both his infant,

Catherine and toddler, Margaret, and their niece and nurse, Katie. Tragically, this nightmare had only just begun.

INVESTIGATIVE LOG ENTRY #1
As reported by The *New York Sun* on August 13:

This place is in a state of intense excitement this morning. Colonel Baker's Union Hotel, near the station, is turned into a temporary hospital, and in the parlors are several of the dead and dying. In the front room lies Mrs. David McCrystal, with her face and body frightfully scalded. By her side is her husband, also severely scalded.

In the next room lies Mrs. Boodle, scalded about the head and face. Near her lies the body of Katie Walsh, aged eleven, who died of her injuries last night. Next to her lies 16-year-old Lillie Grace, seriously burned.

At the neighboring cottages are other victims. At Godfrey Eastlow's, near the hotel, is the infant daughter of the McCrystal's, about four months old, suffering from severe scalds. Another child of the same family is at Mrs. Pearson's close by. This little one, a girl eighteen months old, was in its mother's arms when the collision happened, and the father, snatching it quickly, without waiting to raise the car window, threw it through the window and jumped after it. The baby was afterward picked up only slightly injured and is now doing very well. At the house of Mrs. Smith, near the scene of the accident, is the dead body of Miss Hanratty and two other persons who are suffering from scalds.

The dead body of James Sweeney was sent to Philadelphia this morning. Freddy Carr, four years old, who died soon after the accident and Annie Gillespie, who died early this morning are both at the residence of Mrs. Rape. At a farmhouse near here, Mrs. Mary Waddell of Camden is lying. She is scalded so severely that her life is despaired of.

INVESTIGATIVE LOG ENTRY #2
As reported by The *Mays Landing Record* on August 14:

George Russell, who lives at No. 1304 Belgrade Street, was one of the excursionists. He was on the first train. "We stopped at the station, and had just started when the first thing I knew I saw the train coming. I was standing on the rear platform of the last car on the first section, (next to James Sweeney), and when I saw the train coming I ran to the front of the car and jumped off and waded through the creek. When I looked around I saw the smash.

"The locomotive had run into the car and was in full blaze, while the escaping steam made a frightful noise. The people were all crying and hallooing with pain and fright. Then the town folks came and helped to take the people out of the cars. They were all scalded and hurt. As they were carried out it was a horrible sight."

Estimates on the number of passengers in the last car ranged from 67 to 73, with reports indicating that it was the car with the largest number of infants and children.

The *Catholic Standard* disclosed, "Nearly sixty persons were in the crushed car, and of them, many did not survive." As aid arrived to assist the trapped passengers, it became evident how dire their situation had become. Injury from scalding would render a victim mortally wounded within a day or, more likely, hours.

Father Quinn tended to other severely injured victims with his fellow priests, then sent telegraphic messages of the calamity to St. Anne's, the mayor's office in Philadelphia, and the railroad offices of WJ&A in Camden. He urgently requested a sufficient number of ambulances, up to 35 stretchers to transport the wounded to the hospital, and details of policemen on hand when the train arrived in Camden.

Despite personnel from the Mays Landing station sharing news of the event with the Atlantic City station, it took more than three hours for help to arrive from 17 miles away. Reports later claimed that the urgency of the situation was not conveyed for rail teams to mount an earlier response. As Father Quinn was preparing the wounded for transfer to Philadelphia, he was interrupted by two representatives of Wood's cotton mill, located just a block away. One of whom was a superintendent, George Oatley. Although he did not possess any legal authority, Oatley did all in his power to delay the removal of the injured and dying that night. He was quoted to say, "The laws of New Jersey must be respected." The remarks left the assistant pastor baffled.[3]

Meanwhile, the 5:20 p.m. express, running east from Camden, had arrived at the Mays Landing depot just 200 yards from the collision site. The depot was the scene of utter chaos. On the floors and benches of the waiting room lay the injured, screaming and moaning against the howling outside of what had been described as gale-force winds. Immediately following the mishap, able-bodied passengers were sent about Mays Landing to request aid for the injured.

A gang of the passengers from the wrecked trains saw Conductor Joseph Bartlett who had arrived on the express and came to assist but mistook him for Conductor Hoagland who had jumped seconds before the wreck. They dragged the innocent man off to the nearest telegraph pole and proceeded to tie him up. Shouts for his imminent lynching echoed through the angry mob. Finally, with just moments to spare, his Mays Landing neighbors realized they had captured the wrong conductor and rescued him from near-certain death. Said one angry passenger, "If the wretch had been caught, I wouldn't have given a farthing rushlight for his life. They were after the wretch with clubs and pistols, and I can tell you hot Irish blood wouldn't have stood on much ceremony with such wicked carelessness." Hoagland and Aiken, learning of the threats to their lives, crawled under the train cars, slid down the embankment, and slipped away into the woods. Search parties of several hundred men armed with knives, revolvers, and ropes started in pursuit, but the two had escaped. Returning hours later, a reporter with the *New York Herald* helped the two fugitives hide in the train's baggage car where the frightened men hunkered down until daybreak.

HOTEL LAFAYETTE, THE TOURISTS' HOME, MAYS LANDING, N. J.

THE CHRISTOPHER RAPE HOUSE,
LATER THE HOTEL LAFAYETTE.

Neighbors launched private boats to rescue victims from the swampy waters as others jumped into the river to pull them onto the muddied banks. The wails of the blistered and maimed survivors continued as they were transported to makeshift hospitals, including Colonel Baker's Union Hotel, the American Hotel,[4] the William Moore House, Christopher Rape House and eventually to homes throughout town. The number of passengers on the three trains nearly outnumbered the entire population of Mays Landing. Yet, not enough can be said of the kindness exhibited by the South Jersey community during this ordeal.

Thomas O'Callahan, an organizer with the Excursion Committee, indicated he had been in the rear of the second train. After the shock of the collision, he went about looking for his two children. Once they were found, he tried to pull out as many trapped victims as possible. He went on to describe some of the most frightening images, including a man and woman sitting side by side in their seats, unable to move, surrounded by broken tinder and suffering scalded limbs. Next, he came across a woman with a baby in her arms; both scalded, groaning and crying in constant distress.

Dr. Edward Reichert of Philadelphia had been the only physician on the train. Local citizens, Dr. Denman Ingersoll, county physician, and Dr. Charles Gill, and resident doctor Byron Pennington, a student at Jefferson Medical College in Philadelphia, assisted the most critical cases. However, nothing could have prepared them for the ghastly injuries that they would encounter that night.

With steam temperatures upwards of 200 degrees, dozens suffered from third-degree burns, eventually proving fatal for many. The scalding from the steam in this carnage left some victims in the greatest agony, having their skin dissolved exposing internal wounds and seared lungs caused by inhaling steam. Byron Pennington was said to have found a glove with the flesh and nails of several fingers adhering to it. Some of the victims were so badly scalded that their flesh hung in detached masses from their faces and limbs. Their screams, described in 19th century dialect, were "piercing shrieks of wretched torment."

MINISTERING TO THE DYING

Three people were reported missing and presumed drowned, including sisters Mary and Annie Kelly. Thankfully, news in later days revealed the girls had walked miles from the accident scene and were taken in and returned to the city by a kind-hearted local family. The third missing passenger, Henry Bender, who had escorted his (now deceased) fiancé, Mary Hanratty, on the excursion, was recovered several days later, dead from his injuries.

By modern germ theory of disease, it is possible that treatments rendered to the wounded that evening contributed to more fatalities later due to infection. The disaster scene was tragic as the most severely distressed were readied for their journey home. However, there was no shortage of compassionate aid from the villagers. Local citizens J.P. Walker and Fred Pennington supervised the help as they prepared 30 of the injured for departure. By 11 p.m. that evening, Engine No. 262

was ready for transport to Philadelphia. Three cars from the down express were repositioned while the running engines hummed in preparation for departure from the Mays Landing station. Father Quinn traveled in one of the hospital cars, offering what comfort he could to the sufferers. The near two-hour ride back to Camden was emotionally draining for the grieved pastor. He sat in an exhausted state, listening to the clatter of the wheels on the tracks and the cries of the wounded, all while eyeing the gruesome shadowy figures in the darkness. He listened for the whistles on the steam engines and watched for the ash trail emanating from the fuel source. Then, as his senses sharpened, he prayed for an end to the suffering that was present all around him.

PENNSYLVANIA HOSPITAL, PHILADELPHIA.

INVESTIGATIVE LOG ENTRY #3
As reported by *The Mays Landing Record* on August 14, 1880:

"It was beyond all description to stand on the platform of any one of these cars and glance inside. The forms of the wretched sufferers enveloped in sheets, with their faces as white from the flour[5] sprinkled upon them as their grave-like dress, resembled to many specters; while the strange, unearthly glance of a dome

of impenetrable blackness, added to the illusion of a spectacle so terrible that to have seen it is never to forget it."

Having been kept in suspense for four hours, many of Philadelphia's citizens had not learned of any fatalities until announced by midnight telegraph. Those waiting at home would learn more details from their morning newspapers.

In the city, thousands of panicked family members and friends were held back at Philadelphia's wharf just north of Walnut Street to keep from rushing the cars at Camden's platform. Finally, the train reached the station at approximately 12:45 a.m. as the locomotive No. 262's engine bell tolled once again, announcing their final arrival.

After receiving notice hours prior of the forthcoming wounded, Camden's Chief of Police Givins had commanded all available officers to the pier to secure the wounded. Anticipating the initial numbers to be as high as 200, the chief had summoned additional units, including the Harbor Police, Reserves, and the 2nd, 3rd, and 4th Districts, to standby for receipt of the victims.

The exhausted, weary travelers boarded the ferries at Camden's eastern wharf heading for the opposite shore, ahead of the critical patients and into the waiting arms of their loved ones.

The sufferers were then gingerly removed from the three cars locked and shaded to protect them against gawking onlookers. Emergency units carefully lifted the patients on stretchers and into horse-drawn ambulances to continue to their destination at Spruce and Pine Streets. From half-past one until three o'clock Thursday morning, the massive iron gates to Pennsylvania Hospital's entrance swung open as stretcher after stretcher passed through. The long journey from Atlantic City for the critical 18 men and 12 women was over. The volume of care required for such critical aid delayed patient registrations for several hours following their arrival. Two hospital physicians, Dr. Chapman and Dr. Wetherill, had announced that the chief danger would be the effect of shock more than the burns themselves. In addition, most patients were also seriously affected by the inhalation of steam.

Within hours of reaching the hospital, eight more victims would succumb to their injuries. The average age was 21. Two sisters, preparing for a Christmas reunion with their parents, died within minutes of each other.

Also lost were two mothers and their four daughters ranging in age from 16 to 20 years old. Many more were yet to follow. On the Friday following the crisis, the number of visitors to the Pennsylvania Hospital surged ,with estimates as high as 4,000. August 13, 1880, was recorded as the largest visitor attendance in the hospital's 130-year history. Police were summoned to guard the entrance gates when the hospital decided no further visitors would be granted admission. Hundreds of family, friends, neighbors, and community members gathered on Spruce Street, supporting each other through the days and nights of the crisis.

Of all the heartbreaking stories, particularly tragic was the news that John Grace, father of 16-year-old Lavinia Grace, was denied visitation at the hospital entrance when he was lost among the throngs of people. Later he received word that his youngest daughter had died. He buried her the following Monday without having had the benefit of a final goodbye, while her mother lay in critical condition. He did, however, receive a positive word from the doctor who was attending his eldest daughter Lillie Grace. She was recovering in Mays Landing when it was reported to the devastated father that his daughter's condition was looking hopeful. A very unfortunate error in patient identification. In fact, neither she nor fiancé John Devlin survived their injuries. Lillie's father would not learn the tragic news until he returned to the village of Mays Landing to bring Lillie home to recover. He retraced his journey back to the city that day, tasked with the responsibility of preparing both of his daughters for funerals, while his wife, Elizabeth, lost her battle to this wicked tragedy days later. On Saturday, their families would have been celebrating Lillie and John's wedding.

ATLANTIC COUNTY COURTHOUSE,
MAIN STREET, MAYS LANDING

LET THE INQUESTS BEGIN

On Thursday, dawn of a new day brought more questions than answers on the tragedy 12 hours earlier. Two physicians and six nurses accompanied Father Quinn and Father McBride on the wrecked train back to Mays Landing at 8 a.m. Here, they learned four more young people had succumbed during their absence. With tear-filled eyes, the assistant pastors tried to restrain their emotions as they considered the extent of the losses. They would both have to rely on their faith to carry them through the weeks ahead.

The locomotive and damaged car were promptly removed to Camden and then to upstate Jersey City at approximately 7 a.m., as reported by *The New York Times*.

Dr. Theophilus H. Boysen, a respected physician from Egg Harbor City, held a coroner's inquest after assembling a 10-man jury to convene at 1 p.m. at the Atlantic County Courthouse on Main Street, Mays Landing.

At the depot lay the first casualty, James Sweeney, on the bare floor-boards of a small room without so much as a covering; his horrific injuries exposed while still covered in his blood-stained clothes. Further along Main Street, other victims were more respectfully laid out on ice blocks at Undertaker Champion's Parlor when the jury came

48

in for their review. On the jury were the following local Mays Landing citizens:

- 1. C.E.F. Mayhew, Freeholder for Hamilton Township; Postmaster and shopkeeper of the General Store for the mill.
- 2. Mell Morse
- 3. William Rogers
- 4. William Mattix
- 5. M. Ingrano
- 6 Richard Baxter
- 7. Thomas Kern
- 8. M.R. Peck
- 9. Christopher N. Rape
- 10. Joshua Wilson

That morning Thomas P. Judge of the Excursion Committee for St. Anne's and lawyer for a Philadelphia firm at 520 Walnut Street, had sworn out a warrant before Justice Hoover of Hamilton Township in Mays Landing for carelessness resulting in murder. Mr. Judge petitioned the Justice to hold both men without bail, declaring there were sufficient facts for a clear case against those having charge of the train. The warrant was placed into the hands of the constable, who immediately proceeded to the scene of the wreck and took both men into custody. By 8 a.m., Aiken and Hoagland were apprehended on manslaughter charges, with their bail set at $1,000 each. Members claiming to be Atlantic County's governing body of the Board of Freeholders provided the $2,000 bail bond for the defendants. They were: S. Devenney; Israel S. Adams, son of the WJ&A Director; William Moore, Jr., and George Oatley, the supervisor for Wood's mill.[6]

Atlantic County
Statement of Estimated Expenses for the
year 1880.
Court $4500.
Jail   1500.
Lunatic Asylum   1500.
Board of Officers   800.
Coroner & Physician fees   300.
Elections   300.
Stationery   200.
Advertising & Printing   175.
Incidentals   2500.
Bridges   3000.
Interest on temporary Loans   650
Improvement on Jail   650.
                                    $ 16075.00
Poor   2000.00

A JOURNAL ENTRY IS NOTED FOR $2,500 (INCIDENTAL) FUNDS AND
$2,000 CREDIT FROM THE
ATLANTIC COUNTY FREEHOLDERS ACCOUNT.

General William Sewell, Civil War veteran and New Jersey and former U.S. Senator, had charge of the Camden and Amboy Railroad Company, West Jersey Railroad, and the Camden and Atlantic Railroad Companies. He weighed in on the accident, calling it "criminal recklessness on the part of the engineer." Father McBride of Harrisburg, Pa., stated emphatically that the accident was "surely a result of gross negligence."

Representing the engineer and conductor was local Mays Landing attorney, Joseph (J.E.P.) Abbott of Main Street. This location served as both his business office and his family residence.[7] In his front parlor was an assembly of Mays Landing's male citizens, council representatives, and the accused. Shaking with emotion, Engineer Aiken provided his testimony as he burst into tears recounting the details. Conductor Hoagland shared that he had found the brakes to be in good working order.

The jury also heard from Colonel Joseph Allen, Master of Construction, regarding the grade from Babcock Creek to the Great Egg Harbor River. "At a point on this curve going westward, the grade is thirty-six feet to the mile until it gets on the westerly side of Babcock's Creek. From this point for 600 or 700 feet, it rises between six and seven feet to the mile. From that point to Egg Harbor River is a level grade."[8]

Additionally, Father McBride noted the severe delay, in excess of three hours, of help arriving from Atlantic City.

At approximately 2 p.m., the jury viewed the mortally wounded. Afterward, they began deliberations at 3 p.m. On Friday afternoon, the following day, after three hours of the conference, the jury returned their verdict. Those who were opposed to the degrees of murder charges gradually swayed the others over. They agreed to render the collision and death of James Sweeney accidental and release both men before the end of the day.

Within 24 hours, the two men most responsible for the train wreck and the loss of the passengers were absolved of any culpability for any injury or death.

Aiken and Hoagland quietly toasted their release with dinner at the local tavern, Colonel Baker's Union Hotel, opposite the street from the Mays Landing cotton mill. Inside the same hotel lay three critically ill women, all of whom were slipping away in the most painful suffering. No doubt the screams of the dying disrupted the meal enjoyed by the two accused men.

THE GREATEST LOSS

Anne Gillespie passed away from her injuries without the comfort of her parents by her bedside overnight at the Christopher Rape House, located on another corner of the Mays Landing cotton mill. Resting with her were the remains of Freddy Carr. The five deceased in Mays Landing were not released until the coroner's inquest concluded at 4:45 p.m.

The remains of the dead were transported to the city on the 5:20 p.m. express from Camden. They included 4-year-old Freddy Carr; 11-

year-old Katie Walsh; 12-year-old Anne Gillespie; 20-year-old James Sweeney; and 21-year-old Mary Hanratty.

INVESTIGATIVE LOG ENTRY #4
As reported in *The Times*, Philadelphia on August 14:

The bodies of several victims of the disaster who died from the effects of their injuries have been removed to their homes, whence the funerals will take place.

Little Freddy Carr, the four-year-old son of John J. and Julia Carr will be buried today. The parents are still at the Pennsylvania Hospital, but Mrs. McSorley, a neighbor, has taken charge of their house and has made the arrangements for the funeral.

The funeral of Henry Bender will take place at 1 o'clock Sunday afternoon from No. 1031 East Cumberland Street. Father Kieran from St. Anne's parish will perform the last sad rites and interment will be made at the New Cathedral Cemetery on Nicetown Lane.

Mary Hanratty was accompanied on the ill-fated excursion by Henry Bender. Both lost their lives. The young lady will be buried at 1 o'clock this afternoon from her mother's house on Almendo, above Somerset Street. Father Kieran will perform the funeral services and the interment will be at St. Anne's cemetery.

Mary Green of 828 Wreken Street, will be buried at 3 o'clock tomorrow, Father Kieran will be conducting the funeral services and the interment made at the New Cathedral Cemetery.

The last sad rites will be paid to the body of Joseph McGovern, of 1269 Fisher Street at 10 o'clock Monday morning. The services will be conducted by one of the priests from St. Anne's.

INVESTIGATIVE LOG ENTRY #5
As reported in The *Philadelphia Press* August 15:

"It soon became apparent that many of those who were severely scalded were women. Wives, mothers, sisters and daughters. Anne (age 12 yrs) Gillespie's father would not allow her to travel on previous excursions. According to press accounts, she had Kate Shields, a friend, persuade him to let her go on the trip. Kate, (age 14 yrs) and her sister, Ellen, (age 24 yrs), lived a few houses away.

"Anne was allowed to go and was accompanied to the ferry by her father the next morning, where all three girls set off for the seashore. Anne Gillespie would die early the next morning in Mays Landing. Ellen Shields was at Pennsylvania Hospital. She, too, had received burns on her face, hands, and legs. She would die Friday morning. Kate, her sister, was at Pennsylvania Hospital as well but was not told of Ellen's death, out of fear she might not recover. Kate survived."

The victim's families began the grim task of making funeral arrangements in the cities of both Camden and Philadelphia. The first services occurred at St. Anne's Church for Freddy Carr and Mary Hanratty on Saturday, August 14. James Sweeney and others were buried after Requiem Masses on Sunday and Monday amongst the six area churches. On the following Thursday at 10:30 a.m., a Requiem Mass for the repose of the souls of the victims was celebrated in St. Anne's Church, officiated by the Most Reverend Archbishop James Wood. He delivered the sermon and perform the ceremony of the absolutions with Reverend Mullen and the subdeacon, Father Quinn.

Before the funerals began at St. Anne's Church, seating in the lower half of the center aisle was reserved for the mourning families. Outside, a sea of black consumed the city landscape, reflecting the spiritual darkness and tragic circumstance to their community.

Women wore long black mourning dresses of non-reflective parramatta silk trimmed with crepe. Such attire for the occasion would be without the luxuries that would typically adorn their finery. A widow's bonnet would be made of heavy crepe with a tartan border, and the veil would be worn over the face. Jewelry was limited to 'jet,' a hard, black coal-like material often combined with woven hair of the deceased.

In accordance with Victorian tradition, widows were expected to be in full mourning for two years. A woman wore a mourning dress for one year if she lost a parent or child; six months for a grandparent or sibling. The color of the cloth would lighten as mourning went on from grey to mauve and eventually white. A widower would wear mourning for a year. His mourning would consist of a black suit, black gloves, and necktie. A person in deep mourning would not go into society or receive or pay visits. They would not visit the theater or public places of amusement for six months or more.

Given that most of the victims were from the same Irish neighborhood, grieving customs would dominate many families for months and years to come. The traditions associated with an "Irish wake" would also include celebrating the transition from mortal life to one's arrival in heaven, called the Third Birthday. The first birthday and the second being their actual birthdate and baptism. The "wake home," usually their own, would host viewing by family and friends before the funeral.

Other customs would have included:

- All clocks in the "wake house" stopped at the time of passing.
- Mirrors covered or turned so the soul could easily enter into heaven.
- A pipe was placed on a deceased male's body, along with pipes placed throughout the "wake room." Male visitors might be encouraged to puff the pipes filled with tobacco to discourage visits from "evil spirits" who shy away from smoke.
- The body is draped in white linen with white or black ribbons.
- The body is not left alone. Traditionally a woman would sit with the deceased throughout the waking.
- Crying and wailing, dubbed keening, began after the body was prepared and returned to the "wake home."
- Candles were lit at the foot and head of the deceased.

INVESTIGATIVE LOG ENTRY #6

As reported by *The Philadelphia Inquirer*, August 20, 1880:

The funeral of Catherine, the infant daughter of David and Margarette McCrystal, who died from injuries received at the Mays Landing collision, took place yesterday morning at No. 1922 Edgemont Street. Mrs. Julia Carr, the mother of Little Frederick Carr, who died, is also lying dangerously ill at the Pennsylvania Hospital. There is a slight prospect for her recovery, however.

Scenes envisioned in an Edgar Allan Poe novel played out in homes across the precinct as families received the remains of their loved ones.

In tradition with Victorian custom, many families would have elected to bring a photographer in to memorialize the life of their beloved children, in the form of "after death" or "post mortem" photography. Called "Memento mori Photography," meaning: "remember, you must die," this practice became popular in the mid-to late-19th Century. Often it was the first time families might have had a family photograph taken, particularly those with limited means or in lower-income neighborhoods. Other customs included taking locks off hair cut from the deceased and arranging it to be preserved in lockets, rings, or framed shadow boxes. Death masks were also created in wax as a memento of the life lost. In practices of the "wake," family members would prepare their loved one to receive visitors by washing and dressing their remains in much the same practice as a funeral parlor. The sitting room or "parlor" was arranged for visitation. The funeral service would follow at the church to which the family belonged, usually within three days of the death. Another Victorian mourning practice included "Sunday picnics" at the deceased's cemetery plot. The graveside visits became a weekly practice following Sunday Mass for some families.

Other popular spiritual practices during the Victorian Age were the practices of crystal gazing, seances and the use of Ouija boards, believed to be a potential form of after-death communication.

As the funeral processions proceeded that week, images of black horses and carriages carrying coffin after coffin made melancholy hearts heavier. The crowd outside the church was respectful and orderly due to the police details from the 18th and 24th Districts. Officers assigned to St. Anne's maintained open passage for the cortege and afterward to the cemetery. Most would be interred in the churchyard of St. Anne's, followed by New Cathedral Cemetery, St. Joachim's Cemetery, St. Michael's Cemetery and Newton Cemetery. Several funeral services were held on Saturday and Sunday. Mourning resumed for this Irish Catholic community Monday, August 16.

INVESTIGATIVE LOG ENTRY #7

As reported by *The Camden Morning Post*, August 16:

The scarred bodies of Emma Wright, the mother, and Sarah Wright, the daughter, the wife, and the only child of William Wright, victims of the disaster on the West Jersey and Atlantic City Railroad last Wednesday, were put under the sod in Newton Cemetery yesterday afternoon. They were in the ill-fated car where the steam demon wreaked such havoc, were badly scalded but were brought to their home that night, where Sarah died at 10 o'clock the next morning, followed by the same borne by the mother at 3 o'clock in the afternoon. Unless spirits communicate in the other world, the mother does not know of the death of Sarah. When brought home, they were laid side by side on the same bed of suffering, and when Sarah's pure spirit fled from her pain-racked body, tender hands lifted her lifeless, from the side of the mother who was led to believe that it was being done to ensure more comfort in another room. The mother did not know the daughter was dead. Sarah Wright, aged twenty years, was a member of the Third Street M.E. Church, a consistent Christian, a true, loveable friend, and a gentle, dutiful child, the only one, and the light of the household.

Emma Wright had been a faithful companion, a careful wife for more than a score of years, and the effect of the sudden and tragic loss of both his idols, within such a short time, upon the husband and father, can only be conceived in part.

The funeral was conducted by the undertaker, Frank Middleton, and was announced for 2 o'clock. All the morning, from the early hour, people thronged the neighborhood and a continual stream was passing in to take a look at the scarred faces as they lay by each other's side. When the hour arrived, the streets were packed with humanity, and it was with difficulty that the hearses, containing the remains, could be taken to the Third Street Church, where the services were held.

The daughter was a member and the mother was a regular attendant at the church. The building was packed from the altar to door, the stairs and the vestibules were crowded and a multitude failed even to reach the gate.

The pastor, Dr. J.B. Graw, preached the sermon. What the preacher said and how he said it, can only be conceived by those who have the power to meet an occasion like unto that of yesterday. At the close of the sermon the cortege, consisting of the hearses, twelve carriages bearing the family and friends, a large omnibus drawn by four horses containing the employees at the Camden and

Philadelphia Ferry on which Mr. Wright is a pilot, and a vast concourse of people, left the church and proceeded to Newton Cemetery, when side by side, the mother and daughter will rise together on the resurrection. The stricken husband and father had borne up well, until the clouds rattled upon the caskets hiding the forms of his loved ones, but this doleful sound was too much for him and he was borne, to his home, once so bright, so cheerful, now dark and desolate. Thus was buried Camden's quota, up to the present, to the sad affair. Mrs. Dilkes at 208 Mickle Street, next door to the Wright's, is still living, but this morning there was an increase in fever.

INVESTIGATIVE LOG ENTRY #8

As reported by *Catholic Standard*, Philadelphia, August 21:

"On Monday morning, slow, solemn funeral processions wended their way through the streets to the church and thence to the cemetery. At half-past eight o'clock, the funerals of Rose F. Murphy, aged 21, of Leopard Place, and Kate A., her sister, aged 18, took place from the Church of the Immaculate Conception and were attended by a large number of people.

"The remains of the two sisters encased in black walnut coffins, were placed at the head of the middle aisle and were covered in floral tributes of rich design. The sad scenes of Sunday were repeated at ten o'clock at St. Anne's Church, when Joseph McGovern, 12 years of age, was born from his late home at 1269 Fisher Street. At half-past ten, Sarah Collins, 19 years old, of 229 South Thirteenth Street, was buried from the Church of the Annunciation at 8 o'clock. Mrs. Mary Ann Gallagher, aged 22, of Cumberland and Gaul streets, was buried from her mother's residence, 1141 Ann Street, at 9:30 on Tuesday morning, and Ellen Shields, aged 24, of 1229 Newkirk Street, from St. Anne's Church on Tuesday afternoon at 3 o'clock. The other funerals which followed in the afternoon were those of Mary (Johanna) Green, aged eighteen years, Wreckyn Street above Cedar; Mrs. Margaret McCrystal, aged twenty-seven, from 1922 Edgemont Street and Katie Walsh, aged eleven, from 1921 Edgemont Street-all of which were numerously attended by grieving relatives and friends."

Meanwhile, preparations were underway for a second coroner's inquest in Camden. Testimony of Mays Landing resident and Hamilton Township Assessor, Charles Abbott, claimed he had witnessed the brakes being employed, and the engine reversed. William Walters, a brakeman on the second train, testified that upon hearing the 'down brake' whistle, he attempted to apply the brakes, but it was futile, proving that the brakes were in running order as the automatic Westinghouse Airbrake System was operational. Jacob Mapes, also a brakeman on the second section, testified that the brakes were examined before departing Atlantic City and found all right after being applied just before the collision.

Another witness, Samuel Flower, the fireman on the second section, confirmed the brakes were applied, and the engine reversed. An official from the WJ&A offices in Camden stated that he believed Aiken had done everything he could to stop the train before the collision, although he also had a sense that someone had tampered with the brakes. Samuel Peterman, an Atlantic City policeman, was positive that the first section was not more than 200 yards distant from the second section when the latter left Atlantic City. He also saw the brakes tested, as did Thomas J. Horner, another city policeman. The conductor of the first section, Elmer Mayhew, testified to having no trouble stopping his train with the automatic air brakes. He arrived at Mays Landing at 6:34 p.m., the scheduled time being 6:36 p.m. His train of 16 cars had not passed the switch when the collision occurred.

The second section arrived at the switch a half minute after the first section. It should not have reached that point until four to five minutes later. Conductor Mayhew testified that James Sweeney, the first casualty, was killed almost instantly while standing on the platform of the car struck. His was the last ticket Mayhew had collected just an instant before the collision. Engineer Aiken was then questioned by Coroner William Iszard, investigating the causes that led to the deaths of Mrs. Emma Wright and her 18-year-old daughter, Sarah.

INVESTIGATIVE LOG ENTRY #9

As reported in *The Times,* Philadelphia, August 17:

The Weeping Engineer

All eyes were upon Edward T. Aiken, the engineer of the second section, about whom the most unfavorable comments had been made by the wounded and their friends since the night of the accident.

Upon seating himself in the witness chair, Aiken nervously drew his hand across his eyes to dash away the tears that would now and then trickle down his face, despite all efforts to keep them back. It was a sad tale he had to tell. He told us about him leaving Atlantic City at 6:05, five minutes later than the first section.

"I had no trouble on the way down in the morning," said he. "The air was applied before I left the Excursion House, and on my return the only time I had the occasion to use my air was when I was nearing Mays Landing and there unfortunately I found it didn't work. I was due at Mays Landing at 6:40. I got there at 6:41."

"How was it that you did not get there at 6:40?" asked the Coroner.

Looking up from the floor, where he had kept his eyes since he began his story, he quietly answered, "It was through a little miscalculation."

"Now tell us how your engine became unmanageable?" gently interposed his questioner.

"Well," said Aiken, "when at the top of the hill I was going about twenty five miles an hour. I put the air brake on before I got the curve, but it did no good."

"How was that?"

"I don't know all the checking that was done with the driver-brakes on the engine."

"What brakes were you using?"

"The automatic."

"Where can they be tampered with?"

"Under the cars and in the water closets."

"Did you say anything to your fireman about your inability to stop?"

"I never said a word until I hollered, 'Jump for God's sake, Sam!'"

"Have you ever fired for Cassidy?"

"I have now and then for a day or two at a time."

"Is there any rivalry between you and Cassidy?"

"No, sir, not in the least."

"Are you in the habit of drinking?"

"That's a thing I never do, thank God. They can't lay that on my shoulders."

Here the witness burst out crying afresh. A few minutes elapsed when he was able to reply to the questions put to him by Foreman Cole: *"How fast were you going when you collided with the first train?"*

"No more than three or four miles an hour."

"Do you mean to say you were only going at that slow rate and yet crashed into that car one third of its length?"

"It didn't crash in that distance, but that's the rate I was going at the time."

INVESTIGATIVE LOG ENTRY #10

The following is sworn testimony of Edward T. Aiken, from the Camden County Courthouse, August 17:

George L. Britton: *"What brakes have you been accustomed to using?"*

Edward T. Aiken: *"The Westinghouse."*

Britton: *"What brakes did you use that day?"*

Aiken: *"The automatic."*

Britton: *"How long did you use them previous to that?"*

Aiken: *"I never used them before that day."*

Britton: *"Were you perfectly acquainted with their mode of working?"*

The engineer here put his hand to his forehead and instantly blurted out:

Aiken: *"No, I was not. That's the first day I ever used them, and I didn't apply them properly. I ascertained a few days afterwards from a competent engineer on the Pennsylvania Railroad that I should have kept turning the lever to pump air in the cylinders, whereas I only gave it one turn, as I thought that was sufficient. The automatic is more intricate than the Westinghouse, and I thought all I had to do was to use the former just the reverse of the latter."*

Britton: *"What instructions did you ever get regarding their usage?"*

Aiken: *"The only time I was ever told how to use them was a few minutes before I left the depot yard that morning. I ran up to Dan Cassidy, who was on the engine of the first section, and asked how I should work them. His only reply was "Ed, use them the reverse of the Westinghouse.""*

Britton: *"So that's all the instructions you ever received?"*

Aiken: *"Yes sir, that's all."*

In a few words, Aiken stated that he had undertaken to use the automatic brakes for the first time on the day of the accident. He had no prior experience with the system, and, at the critical moment, he failed to stop the train. His admission was shocking and unexpected. For a moment, the silence was broken only by the engineer's sobs. He broke down completely and was sent from the room.

INVESTIGATIVE LOG ENTRY #11

As reported in *The Times*, Philadelphia, August 17:

"These admissions by Aiken seemed to make a deep impression upon all present. Such a turn of events had not been expected. Turning to Coroner Iszard, the witness said the only occasion he had to use the brakes previously was on his down trip, on entering Mays Landing and while approaching Pomona and when hauling up at Atlantic City. At three points he gave himself plenty of room to use his driver brakes. Neither the Coroner nor the jury seemed disposed to further question the witness, so he was told he might go for the present, but to still consider himself under oath until recalled to the stand."

INVESTIGATIVE LOG ENTRY #12

As reported in *The New York Sun*, August 25:

The Coroner's Jury at Camden, N.J., after hearing the testimony of twenty-eight witnesses concerning the Mays Landing disaster, retired at 10 o'clock last night and returned a verdict this morning. They say they find that the automatic brake used by the West Jersey and Atlantic Company is the best in use for the safety of public travel. As to the collision the jury makes the following remarks: "We do further find that the cause of said collision was occasioned by a combination of circumstances. First, the unfavorable condition of the rails of the said West Jersey and Atlantic, occasioned by recent rains, greatly enhanced the collision; second, the limited time allowed between the starting of the first and second sections of the excursion train; third, the inability of the engineer having in charge engine No. 627, drawing the said second section to manage the automatic brake with which said train was provided or from some unforeseen cause to this jury unknown."

A third jury from the Philadelphia Inquest agreed that the collision and resulting deaths were accidental. William Richard, the foreman of engines stated that if the throttle valve of the engine had been closed the steam would not have escaped. A severely scalded passenger, Thomas J. McGrath, from Port Richmond, testified that he felt, "a terrible crashing of timber and ironwork all around him followed by the rushing of the steam." He was quoted to say, "As an old railroad man, I feel almost positive that the engineer of the approaching train did not 'shut off'" up to the time of the accident. Because of the cylinders, if the engine burst, the steam having free vent poured out in torrents with the scalding water into the car. Had the throttle valve been closed, it could not have escaped." As a sufferer of a lung infection, his hacking in the courtroom between sentences gave way to a bloodied cough. He took out his tattered hanky in an attempt to quiet the nuisance but the burden of his scalding injuries had left him in the poorest health. So he could testify, his kind neighbor, Mrs. McSorley, escorted him to the city's courthouse and back to his River Ward neighborhood. He died from his combined injuries later that night.

The next witness, Assistant Trainmaster, M. Mills, testified that the airbrake had undoubtedly been tampered with, either by accident or design, he could not say. It was his opinion that someone must have put it out of order by fooling with it in one of the closets, in one of the cars through which it passes, stating: "Westinghouse is the very best air brake system in use."

The grand jury reconvened on September 14, 1880. Their first order was to assemble in the train yard in Jersey City, where the wrecked engine and car had been removed 32 days prior. Both the engine and the car were found to have minimal damage, indicating a low rate of speed at the time of impact. Examination of the track at Mays Landing proved it to be equipped with all the modern equipment in safe railroading. Among the members sitting on the jury was Israel Guthrie Adams, son of the director of the WJ&A and sole jury member from Atlantic County. Israel, Sr., was considered one of the wealthiest and most influential men in South Jersey, owning numerous merchant ships and large parcels of real estate. Upon receiving their instructions, the jury was advised:

If the death of a passenger occurred as a result of carelessness, or if an incompetent man was placed in charge of a train with the same result, the employee AND company official would be rendered guilty of manslaughter.

Eight months earlier, on Dec. 29, 1879, George Wood had signed an operating agreement giving West Jersey "full and exclusive power, right and authority" to operate the WJ&A when completed.

In all, 24 witnesses testified over four days. Despite overwhelming evidence proving negligence, the collision was ruled accidental, rendering no one accountable by unanimous verdict. By the date of the final inquest, 16 claims were already being represented by lawyers. Settlements for each of the deaths by WJ&A averaged $500 per person. In today's dollars, the settlements would equal just $13,090.

By Feb. 23, 1881, all claims from the accident had been settled, totaling $82,500, or $2,159,995 in today's dollars. The amount was classified as an operating expense.

WHAT THE JURIES NEVER LEARNED[9]:

1. By May of 1880, before the June launch, the WJ&A had already had two derailments due to poorly aligned tracks.

2. The number of coaches on the August 11 excursion was inadequate for the number of passengers traveling.

3. Operating costs had consumed all the revenue and kept the WJ&A from being financially successful, as reported in meeting minutes.

4. The superintendent of the mill mysteriously delayed the passenger's return to Philadelphia on two separate occasions.

5. The excursion coordinators desired to run a single consist to Atlantic City round trip. The PRR, who oversaw the Camden operations, insisted they would be running two separate trains that day, despite known hazards.

6. The site of the collision and the Mays Landing cotton mill's loading dock were within one block of each other and ran under the same management company.

7. The journal entry for the $2,000 funds withdrawn from the Atlantic County Freeholders' accounts for Bail Bonds was recorded as an "incidental" expense. No further explanation was offered. The funds were quietly taken and quietly replaced.

8. Names of four Freeholders provided to the press by WJ&A were not actually Freeholders: Solomon Devenney; William Moore Jr., Israel Adams, Jr.; and George Oatley, supervisor at Wood's cotton mill.

9. The Freeholder, Charles Mayhew, who arranged the bail bond for Aiken and Hoagland was also an employee of the Wood mill, working in the general store. He served as foreman for the jury in Mays Landing.

10. Archbishop James Wood of the Philadelphia diocese helped coordinate the excursion and also presided over funerals of the accident victims.

11. Despite 10 deaths occurring in Mays Landing, all death records are recorded in Philadelphia.

What Happened to Them?

Engineer Edward Aiken had a wife and three children, at 526 Bridge Street, Camden. He was acquitted of all counts; his whereabouts afterward were never known.

Joseph Bartlett, Jr., a conductor on the Camden and Atlantic Railroad. A member of the Unity Lodge No. 96, he served as Worshipful Master in 1882, 1887, and 1906. He also served one term as Atlantic County Sheriff during World War I. He is buried in Mays Landing Presbyterian Cemetery on Route 50.

Conductor Charles Hoagland, 510 Federal Street, Camden, continued to work on the Camden-Cape May Express until he passed away from tuberculosis in 1909.

Father Francis Quinn, After taking command of the event, continued to comfort his parishioners at St. Anne's and serve his congregation for the next 25 years.

George Wood returned to the Millville Manufacturing Company as president after the accident and remained active in his community. He also served on the Board of Directors of the Millville National Bank, and was an incorporator of the South Jersey Traction Company, providing trolley service between Millville, Bridgeton, and Vineland. In later years, he led a quiet life on his Pennsylvania dairy farm until his death in 1926. He is buried in a modest plot in Laurel Hill Cemetery, Philadelphia, overlooking Lehigh Ave, only a few blocks from St. Anne's Church and her many lost souls.

Throughout the weeks that followed, compliments were extended about the kindness provided to the victims by the people of Mays Landing. From funeral masses to national and international press, Father Thomas Kieran of St. Anne's went so far as to say, "There never were more charitable people." Passenger John Matthews spoke warmly of the attention paid to the wounded by the people of Mays Landing and by the physicians who were hastily called to the disaster scene.

A victim with his head swathed in cotton stated, "Why, they couldn't have been kinder to us if we had been their own people. Flour, linseed oil, blankets, and everything that was asked for was forthcoming. They did all they could." Furthermore, the president of St. Ann's Literary Institute, Thomas Judge, remarked, "The people here have done everything that could be done for the wounded. Every person who could render aid offered it gladly, and there was no lack of tender care."

Afterwards

By the return of the workweek after the event, citizens of Mays Landing were back to work at the cotton mill. Generations of families remained dedicated to the town's largest employer until it closed in 1949. Eventually, the company store and coal yard would become Unity Lodge No. 96, still standing today, as is the company's schoolhouse, now home to the Hamilton Historical Society and Museum.

Had it been properly recorded, by today's standards, the disaster on the WJ&A at Mays Landing would rank as one of the deadliest train collisions in New Jersey's rail history. Some events in history are shadows in time; long overdue for reflection for the innocent lives lost and those that were forever changed.

The WJ&A was in its first season of service when it was confronted with a horrific tragedy and public relations nightmare.

With many young victims having immediate family overseas, claims were settled and cases closed while the news was still reaching their homeland in Ireland. In exerting 'damage control' by moving the process quickly along, the railroad was able to salvage the WJ&A and quell the outcry that most certainly would have ensued. The season change allowed time for the company to regroup and essentially redirect the news cycle.

Although press coverage in the South Jersey area was elusive, New Jersey media outlets included papers in the towns of Passaic, Newark, Red Bank, and Freehold. Nearly 40 newspapers in the state of Kansas covered the story. Details of the accident including victims' names, addresses, and the severity of their injuries or loss of life were reported in the following U.S. cities. This is just a sampling of the thousands of readers nationwide who were informed of this tragedy in Mays Landing:

Arkansas Democrat, Little Rock, Ark.
Oakland Tribune, Oakland, Calif.
San Francisco Chronicle, San Francisco, Calif.
Hartford Courant, Hartford, Conn.
The Daily Gazette, Wilmington, Del.
National Republican, Washington D.C.
The Atlanta Constitution, Atlanta, Ga.
Chicago Tribune, Chicago, Ill.
The Pantagraph, Bloomington, Ill.
Knoxville Whig and Chronicle, Knoxville, Ill.
Angola Herald, Angola, Ind.
Warrenton Gazette, Warrenton, Ind.
Bristol Banner, Bristol, Ind.
Fort Wayne Daily Gazette, Fort Wayne, Ind.
Sioux City Journal, Sioux City, Iowa
Quad City Times, Davenport, Iowa
The Times, Clay Center, KS
Blue Rapid Terms, Blue Rapids, Kan.
McPherson Freeman, McPherson, Kan.
Fort Scott Daily Monitor, Fort Scott, Kan.
The St. John Weekly News, St. John, Kan.
Western Home Journal, Lawrence, Kan.
The Valley Republican, Kinsley, Kan.
Kansas State Journal, Topeka, Kan.
Chase County Leader, Cottonwood Falls, Kan.
The Head-Light, Thayer, Kan.
Madison News, Madison, Kan.
Harper County Times, Harper, Kan.
The Moline News, Moline, Kan.
Lawrence Daily Journal, Lawrence, Kan.
The Oneida Journal, Oneida, Kan.
The Daily Commonwealth, Topeka, Kan.
Nemaha County Republican, Sabetha, Kan.
The Selinsgrove Times, Selinsgrove, Kan.
The Independent, Riley, Kan.
The Garnett Republican, Garnett, Kan.
Millbrook Times, Millbrook, Kan.

Sterling Kansas Bulletin, Sterling, Kan.

Minneapolis Independent, Minneapolis, Kan.

The Ellinwood Express, Ellinwood, Kan.

Cawker City Public Record, Cawker City, Kan.

The Ottawa Daily Weekly, Ottawa, Kan.

Atchison Champion, Atchison, Kan.

The Junction City Tribune, Junction City, Kan.

The Miami Republican, Paola, Kan.

Kansas Valley Times, Rossville, Kan.

The Caldwell Commercial, Caldwell, Kan.

Linn County Clarion, Mound City, Kan.

The Times, Shreveport, La.

The Times Democrat, New Orleans, La.

The Baltimore Sun, Baltimore, Md.

Fall River Daily Herald, Fall River, Mass.

Boston Post, Boston, Mass.

Boston Globe, Boston, Mass.

The Palmyra Spectator, Palmyra, Mo.

St. Louis Post Dispatch, St. Louis, Mo.

St. Louis Globe Democrat, St. Louis, Mo.

The Kansas City Times, St. Joseph, Mo.

Nebraska State Journal, Lincoln, Neb.

The Opposition, Crete, Neb.

Lincoln Daily Globe, Lincoln, Neb.

The Weekly State Democrat, Lincoln, Neb.

The Brooklyn Daily Eagle, Brooklyn, N.Y.

Catholic Union and Times, Buffalo, N.Y.

The Sun, New York, N.Y.

The New York Tribune, New York, N.Y.

The New York Times, New York, N.Y.

Weekly New Mexican, Santa Fe, N.M.

Lancaster Intelligencer, Lancaster, Pa.

The Inquirer, Philadelphia, Pa.

Daily Independent, Harrisburg, Pa.

York Gazette, York, Pa.

Scranton Republican, Scranton, Pa.

Pittsburgh Daily Post, Pittsburgh, Pa.

The Altoona Tribune, Altoona, Pa.
Harrisburg Telegraph, Harrisburg, Pa.
The Philadelphia Inquirer, Philadelphia, Pa.
Reading Times, Reading, Pa.
Record of the Times, Wilkes Barre, Pa.
The Times, Philadelphia, Pa.
Knoxville Daily Chronicle, Knoxville, Tenn.
Austin Weekly Statesmen, Austin, Texas
Dallas Daily Herald, Dallas, Texas
Memphis Daily Appeal, Memphis, Tenn.
Richmond Dispatch, Richmond, Va.
Rutland Daily Herald, Rutland, Vt.
The Poultney Journal, Poultney, Vt.
Burlington Free Press, Burlington, Vt.
The Salt Lake Herald, Salt Lake City Utah
Wood County Reporter, Grand Rapids, Wis.
The Oshkosh Evening Star, Oshkosh, Wis.
The Richmond Dispatch, Richmond, Va.
Wheeling Daily Intelligencer, Wheeling, W.Va.

June 21.—Atlantic express north, conductor J. S. Mikesner and engineer T. Bodell, struck and instantly killed Thomas N. Hammond, near Temperanceville road crossing.

July 10.—A passenger named Edward Hall, fell off Atlantic express north, (conductor E. G. Blaisdell, and engineer D. Cassady,) at Marlboro " Y," and was slightly injured.

July 15.—Thomas Quinn was found lying near the track unconscious, about 300 yards north of Gloucester, with one leg cut off. Supposed to have been struck by Woodbury accommodation north. Conductor F. Simkins; engineer W. C. Scott.

August 2.—John Pearson, a brakeman on Cape May freight, (conductor F. Mount, and engineer D. Leeds,) had his right arm badly crushed while drilling at Millville.

August 5.—Atlantic express south, conductor C. P. Mikesner, and engineer J. Griner, struck and instantly killed Elizabeth Young, about 100 yards north of Stockton Station.

August 9.—Woodbury accommodation north, conductor F. Simkins, and engineer W. C. Scott, struck and severely injured Mrs. Randall Morgan, at Second street crossing, Camden.

September 1.—A colored man, named Douglas Smith, was found in rear car of excursion train on arrival at Camden, with skull fractured. Cause of accident was never ascertained. Conductor J. C. Sweeten, and engineer T. Clayton.

September 14.—Benjamin Packer, baggage-master on Cape May express north, was struck by Westville bridge and fatally injured, while leaning out side door of car. Conductor H. C. Mulliner, and engineer D. Focer.

September 30.—Cape May express north, conductor A. L. Sparks and engineer S. Chester, struck and instantly killed Mrs. Jane Knight at Central avenue crossing, South Camden.

November 16.—Wenonah accommodation north, conductor W. _____ _____ _____ Cassady, struck and severely injure

THE 1880 NEW JERSEY RAILROAD AND CANAL REPORT,
IN THE STATE ARCHIVES IN TRENTON,
LISTS NO INCIDENT ON AUGUST 11, 1880.

- Feb. 20, 1880 Camden & Atlantic Railroad holds excursion to showcase new Woodruff parlor car Marion F. (RyW)

- Feb. 25, 1880 Committee of West Jersey Railroad Board reports in favor of accepting proposition of Five Mile Beach Improvement Company to build railroad to Anglesea. (MB)

- Feb. 26, 1880 Jay Gould proposes to sell Vineland Railway (Atsion-Bayside, N.J.) to PRR and detach it from CNJ system, eliminating competition with West Jersey Railroad; PRR accepts, but Gould is unable to deliver, the move being a bluff in his negotiations with the CNJ. (MB)

- Feb. 27, 1880 West Jersey Railroad Board hears offer of Camden, Gloucester & Mt. Ephraim Railway to sell. (MB)

- Mar. 18, 1880 Camden & Atlantic Railroad Board reports that Mays Landing & Egg Harbor City Railroad is in bad shape and should give up lease of extension from Mays Landing station to shipyard as soon as possible; vote to continue trains on Atlantic Avenue in Atlantic City, as residents demand it; report that PRR refuses to join in buying Philadelphia & Atlantic City Railway, and Massey has increased his price from $390,000 to $420,000. (MB)

- Apr. 15, 1880 Camden & Atlantic Railroad Board orders opening new slips at Camden with trial run of new ferry Atlantic; new station is almost completed. (MB,PubLdgr)

- Apr. 1880 Anglesea Railroad signs construction contract with Peter F. Collins of Philadelphia. (RRG)

- Apr. 25, 1880 Camden & Atlantic Railroad begins running seasonal Sunday express train between Camden and Atlantic City. (PubLdgr)

-

- Jan. 10, 1898 Removal of Smith and Windmill Islands in Delaware River completed. (Boyer)

THE WEST JERSEY & ATLANTIC RAILROAD TIMELINE, IN THE STATE
ARCHIVES IN TRENTON,
LISTS NO INCIDENT ON AUGUST 11, 1880.

Today, no official record of an incident or mishap occurring at Mays Landing on August 11, 1880, is on file with these offices or agencies:

1. Annual Statement of Railroads and Canals of the State of New Jersey 1880, Trenton.

2. National Railroad Historical Society, Moorestown, N.J.

3. West Jersey Chapter of National Railroad Historical Society, Palmyra, N.J.

4. Railroad Museum of Pennsylvania, Strasburg, Pa.

In May 1896, West Jersey experienced another collision and boiler explosion. The accident killed 50 and seriously injured 60 passengers in Atlantic City.

October 1906 saw a third major accident, this one on the newly constructed bridge into Atlantic City when its failure to close sent the train cars plummeting into 30 feet of water below, drowning fifty-three people. The accident resulted in what is regarded as the first press release. Public relations expert Ivy Lee, employed with the Pennsylvania Railroad and parent company of the West Jersey and Seashore Railroad, persuaded the management to present a statement to journalists at the scene of the accident. Many outlets printed the release word-for-word on Oct. 30, 1906.

In December 1950, the West Jersey Line was abandoned from Newfield to Mays Landing. In August 1966, the segment to McKee City was formally abandoned, ending the rail era in Mays Landing.

Intentions for 27.2-mile "Bikeway East" on West Jersey's railbed had it linking from Egg Harbor Township to Hamilton Township's Gaskill Park in Mays Landing as the first phase. "Bikeway West," through western Atlantic County, had been planned for 1992, but funding and a challenging course put the plans on indefinite hold. By early 2001, county freeholders announced project costs had ballooned to almost $900,000 with an indefinite completion.

In 2021, following the year of the pandemic, South Jersey Transportation Planning Organization and Atlantic County took a renewed interest in the Atlantic County Bikeway West. In conducting a feasibility study to close the 16-mile gap in South Jersey's Trail Network between Atlantic and Camden counties, the first steps towards a possible redevelopment of Mays Landing's train station and the West Jersey rail corridor are once again under consideration for 2022.

THE TRESTLE OF THE WJ&A LINE REMAINS.

West of the station, the remnants of the trestle bridge span the Great Egg Harbor River, a favorite fishing destination for the past 50 years. The surface of the bridge was badly damaged by Hurricane Sandy in 2012, leaving little but the trestle supports jutting from the riverbed. In its eerie appearance, it has quietly held over a century of secrets and dreams of the innocents who were lost too soon one stormy summer night, somewhere between the Shore and the City.

VOICE FOR THE VICTIMS

Casualties from August 11, 1880, Mays Landing Tragedy:
Injured
James Bender
Mrs. Ellen Bodell, 42 years
Patrick Bowen
Robert Bowen
Patrick Brown
Henry Carr, 35 years
John Carr, 30 years
Julia Carr, 33 years
Kate Carr
Angelina Clifton
John Conlon
Josephine Delty, 19 years
John Devan
Sarah Devlin
Georgianna Dilkes, 40 years
Mrs. Dill
John Doran, 21 years
Joseph Durks
Julia Durks
Fanny Fenton
Thomas Fitch
Tom Fitzpatrick, 28 years
Johanna Grace
John Grace
Mary Grace
Libby Grier
Leon Hartley
Mary Kurtz
Patrick McArran, 21 years
Mary McConnel
Mary McCormick
David McCrystal
Mary McDevitt

Patrick McDevitt
Patrick McDonnell
Ellen McGonigle
Harry McKey
Katy McKinsey
Thomas McLintall
Catherine McLaughlin
Ellen McMonigle
Ella McMorgan
Francis Mullen
James Mullen, 25 years
Thomas Murphy
Margaret O'Donnell
Henry Ratsy
Samuel Sayers
Kate Shields, 13 years
Frederick Shower
Margaret Smith, 46 years
Mary Smith, 40 years old
Michael Smith, 40 years
Patrick Smith, 47 years
Alexander Sweeney
Thomas Timlin, 17 years
Thomas Turlan
Mary Waddell
William Walsh
William Wright

Died in Camden
Emma Wright, 35 years
Sarah Wright, 19 years

Died at Mays Landing
Freddy Carr 4 years
Annie Gillespie, 12 years
Lillie Grace, 19 years
Mary J. Green, 17 years
Mary Hanratty, 22 years
Margarette McCrystal, 27 years

James Sweeney, 20 years
Kate Walsh, 11 years
Died in Pennsylvania
Henry Bender, 23 years
Sarah Collins, 23 years
John Devlin, 25 years
Charles Frost, 28 years
William Frost
Mary Ann Gallagher
Will Gallagher, 25 years
Elizabeth Grace
Livinia Grace, 17 years
Patrick McBride, 24 years
Henry McCann, 26 years
Catherine McCrystal, 20 months
Margaret McCrystal, 4 months
Mary McDonald
Joseph McGovern, 12 years
Thomas McGrath, 40 years
Kate Murphy, 22 years
Rose Murphy, 19 years
Ellen Shields, 24 years
Owen Walsh, 18 years

THE GREAT EGG HARBOR RIVER.

In Remembrance

This account of events is dedicated to the 60 passengers critically injured and the 30 souls lost, as a result of the tragedy at Mays Landing. Their story has finally been told.

"Sleep in heavenly peace."

Mari D'Albora Dattolo

NOTES

CHAPTER 1

1. Now the Unity Lodge.
2. $2,002,905 in today's dollars.

CHAPTER 3

1. 2,600 feet equals ½ mile.
2. The depot was located where Mays Landing Firehouse is now situated.
3. Research with the state archives indicates that none of the deaths occurring in New Jersey had been issued state Death Certificates. However, further investigation with St. Anne's records finds that certification of some form had been provided for burial.
4. Now the Atlantic County Library System Headquarters.
5. Flour was used to soothe burned skin.
6. Research has confirmed that none were then Freeholders, nor had they ever been.
7. Now The Abbott House.
8. 36 ft to the mile is about 1/2 of a percent grade; grades in America are generally 1 percent or less.
9. Reference includes PRR Meeting Minutes & Research

ACKNOWLEDGMENTS

Professional Sources
With Appreciation & Thanks,
I. McMichael, President, 2018-19, Township of Hamilton Historical Society, Mays Landing
J. Craddock, Vice President 2018-, Township of Hamilton Historical Society
C. Farrell, Curator, Township of Hamilton Historical Museum, Mays Landing
P. Farrell Joseph, Genealogist
L. Wood, Historian, Greater Egg Harbor Township Historical, Atlantic County Historical Society, Somers Point
P. Saunders, Research Atlantic County Library, Mays Landing
L. Clark, Research, New Jersey State Library, Trenton
A. DiGiovanni, Editor, Historical Society of Pennsylvania, Philadelphia
J. Hohenstein, Research, Jenkins Law Library, Philadelphia
F. Niven, Editor, PR Council for Atlantic City
W. Jennings, Retiree, Locomotive and Train Mechanical Safety OPS
J. Piggott, Rail Historian, Cape May County
L. Dean, Research, National Rail History Society PHL

W.G. Cook, Author, Atlantic City Railroad
J. Burlage, Research, West Jersey Chapter (NRHS)
L. Radkiew, Research, Rail Museum of Pennsylvania, Strasburg, Pa.
D. Niceler, Rail Historian, Egg Harbor City Historical Museum
L. Ferrero, Curator, St. Anne's Historical Committee, Philadelphia
R. Francois, Curator, Wood Mansion & Millville Historical Society
S. Peeples, Curator, Pennsylvania Hospital, Philadelphia
S. Besserman, Film Maker, AriJoe Productions
M. Gilliano, Conductor, Reenactor for Events
A. Lewis Korth, Train Wreck Victim, Reenactor for Events
K. Dalbora, Investigator, Philadelphia Locations
L. Dalbora, Investigator, Millville Locations
M. Dare, Investigator, Florence Location
W. Fabietti, Innkeeper, Inn at Sugar Hill, Mays Landing
S. Brentari, Founder, *Jersey Shore Family* magazine, Mays Landing
M. Phy, GEHR Photo Credit 7/21

In the course of conducting research, the author also visited the Laurel Hill Cemetery, Philadelphia, and the New Jersey State Archives, Trenton.

Bibliography

"Accidental." *The Philadelphia Inquirer* [Philadelphia], 14 8 1880, p. 1. *Newspapers.com*. Accessed 2018.

"After The Wreck." *Courier-Post* [Camden, NJ], 13 8 1880, p. 1. *Newspapers.com*. Accessed 2018.

Aldrich, Mark. *Death Rode the Rails American Railroad Accidents and Safety 1828-1965*. Baltimore, Johns Hopkins University Press, 2006.

"Another Catholic Disaster." *Knoxville Daily Chronicle* [Knoxville, TN], 14 8 1880, p. 1. *Newspapers.com*. Accessed 2018.

"Atlantic City via 'The Old Reliable.'" *The Times* [Philadelphia], 17 8 1880, p. 1. *Newspapers.com*. Accessed 2018.

"Bail is Set." *The Times* [Philadelphia], 13 8 1880, p. 1. *Newspapers.com*. Accessed 2019.

Burgess, George. *Centennial History of the Pennsylvania Railroad Company 1846-1946*. Philadelphia, University of Pennsylvania Press, 1949.

The Catholic Standard. "Burying the Dead." *The Catholic Standard* [Philadelphia], 21 8 1880, p. 1.

"The Cause of the Mays Landing Accident." *The Sun* [New York], 17 8 1880, p. 1. Accessed 2018.

"Church Announces Changes." *The Times* [Philadelphia], 17 8 1880, p. 1. *Newspapers.com*. Accessed 2018.

Churella, Albert J. *The Pennsylvania Railroad-Building an Empire 1846-1917*. vol. Vol 1, University of Pennsylvania, 2012.

Clark, Dennis. *The Irish in Philadelphia*. Philadelphia, Temple University Press, 1973.

"The Collision at Mays Landing." *The New York Times* [New York], 22 8 1880, p. 1. *Newspapers.com*. Accessed 2018.

"The Collision on the Atlantic City Railroad." *The Dallas Daily Herald* [Dallas, TX], 14 8 1880, p. 1. *Newspapers.com*. Accessed 2018.

Cook, W. G. *Atlantic City Railroad The Royal Route to the Sea*. Ambler, PA, Crusader Press, 1980.

Czachowski, Joe. *Historic Photos of Jersey Shore*. New Jersey, Turner Publishing, 2007.

"The Deadly Rail." *Detroit Free Press* [Detroit], 13 8 1880, p. 1. *Newspapers.com*. Accessed 2019.

"Died." *The Philadelphia Inquirer* [Philadelphia], 13 8 1880, p. 1. *Newspapers.com*. Accessed 2018.

"Died." *The Philadelphia Inquirer* [Philadelphia], 20 8 1880, p. 1. *Newspapers.com*. Accessed 2018.

"Died." *The Philadelphia Inquirer* [Philadelphia], 17 9 1880, p. 1. *Newspapers.com*. Accessed 2018.

Diner, Hasia R. *Erin's Daughters in America*. Baltimore, The John Hopkins University Press, 1983.

Domino, Gabriel. *Garment Workers of South Jersey*. Stockton University, 2016.

Duffy, Edward W. *Philadelphia: A Railroad Story*. Philadelphia, Camino Books, Inc., 2013.

"The Engineer and Conductor." *The Times* [Philadelphia], 13 8 1880, p. 1. *Newspapers.com*. Accessed 2018.

"Fixing the Blame." *The Philadelphia Inquirer* [Philadelphia], 17 8 1880, p. 1. *Newspapers.com*. Accessed 2018.

Forgotten Books, editor. *Atlantic City, New Jersey Camden and*

Atlantic Railroad Company, to the Sea-Shore. London, J. B. Lippincott and Co., 2018.

Funnell, Charles. *By The Beautiful Sea-The Rise and High Times of that Great American Resort, Atlantic City.* Alfred A. Knopf, Inc., 197"Getting at the Facts." *The Philadelphia Inquirer* [Philadelphia], 19 8 1880, p. 1. *Newspapers.com.* Accessed 2018.

"Getting at the Truth." *The Times* [Philadelphia], 17 8 1880, p. 1. *Newspapers.com.* Accessed 2018.

Haine, Edgar A. *Railroad Wrecks.* Cranbury, NJ, Rosemont Publishing, 1993.

Historical Society, Twsp Hamilton of. *Township of Hamilton, Atlantic County.* Mays Landing, NJ, Arcadia Publishing, 2001.

"How the Railroads Created Atlantic City." *NJSpotlight.com,* http://www.njspotlight.com/stories/18/08/26/summer-reading-how-the-rr-created-atlantic-city/. Accessed 18 3 2019.

"An Inquest." *Fort Scott Daily Monitor* [Fort Scott, Kansas], 14 8 1880, p. 1. *Newspapers.com.* Accessed 2018.

"The Jury Out." *Courier-Post* [Camden, NJ], 21 8 1880, p. 1. *Newspapers.com.* Accessed 2018.

"Many People Injured." *The Times* [Philadelphia], 12 8 1880, p. 1. *Newspapers.com.* Accessed 2018.

"The Mays Landing Collision." *The Charlotte Observer* [Charlotte, NC], 24 8 1880, p. 1. *Newspapers.com.* Accessed 2018.

"The Mays Landing Disaster." *The Sun* [New York], 25 8 1880, p. 1. *Newspapers.com.* Accessed 2018.

"Mays Landing Disaster." *Passaic Daily News* [Passaic], 13 8 1880. *Newspapers.com.* Accessed 2019.

"Mays Landing Horror." *Harrisburg Independent* [Harrisburg, PA], 13 8 1880, p. 1. *Newspapers.com.* Accessed 2018.

"Mays Landing Inquest." *The Philadelphia Inquirer* [Philadelphia], 18 8 1880, p. 1. *Newspapers.com.* Accessed 2018.

"Mays Landing: Number of Deaths Increase." *Record of the Times* [Wilkes Barre-PA], 14 8 1880, p. 1. *Newspapers.com.* Accessed 2018.

Mazzagetti, Dominick. *The Jersey Shore.* New Brunswick, NJ, Rutgers University Press, 2018.

Michael, Bibel. *Train Wreck: The Forensics of Rail Disasters.* Baltimore, John Hopkins University Press, 2012.

"The New Jersey Railroad Disaster." *The Burlington Free Press* [Burlington, VT], 13 8 1880, p. 1. *Newspapers.com*. Accessed 2018.

"The News is Tragic." *The Philadelphia Inquirer* [Philadelphia], 13 8 1880, p. 1. *Newspapers.com*. Accessed 2018."NJ Railroad Collision." *Angola Herald* [Angola, Ind.], 18 8 1880, p. 1. *Newspapers.com*. Accessed 2018.

"Obituaries." *The Philadelphia Inquirer*, 13 8 1880, p. 1. *Newspapers.com*. Accessed 2018.

O'Dowd, Niall. *Lincoln and the Irish*. New York, Skyhorse Publishing, 2018.

"Particulars of the West Jersey Railroad Disaster." *The Brooklyn Daily Eagle* [Brooklyn, N.Y.], 12 8 1880, p. 1. *Newspapers.com*. Accessed 2018.

"Rail Disaster in N.J." *The Blue Rapids Times* [Blue Rapids, KS], 19 8 1880, p. 1. *Newspapers.com*. Accessed 2018.

"Railway Inquests Continue." *Bristol Banner* [Bristol, IN], 20 8 1880, p. 1. *Newspapers.com*. Accessed 2018.

"Railway Slaughter." *Boston Post* [Boston, MA], 13 8 1880, p. 1. *Newspapers.com*. Accessed 2018.

Reed, Robert C. *Train Wrecks A Pictorial History of Accidents on the Main Line*. New York, Bonanza Books, 1953.

Scull, Kenneth. "Dateline: Mays Landing The Mays Landing-Egg Harbor Railroad." *Atlantic County Record* [Mays Landing], 3 October 1974, p. 1.

Shinn, Robert A. *Along the Cooper River*. Charleston, SC, Arcadia Publishing, 2014.

Siegel, Alan A. *Disaster! Stories of Destruction and Death in Nineteenth-Century New Jersey*. New Brunswick, New Jersey, Rutgers University Press, 2014.

Sievers, Bruce R. *Mills Along The River*. Moodus, Moodus Printing & Graphics, 1985.

Simonsen, Mary L. *The mud Run Train Wreck*. Peoria, AZ, Quail Creek Publishing, 2015.

"Summer Reading 2018: How the Railroads Created Atlantic City." *NJ Spotlight*, 2018, p. 5. https://www.njspotlight.com/stories/18/08/26/summer-reading-2018-how-the-rr-created-atlantic-city/. Accessed 2019.

"Terrible Accident." *Daily Journal* [Vineland], 12 8 1880, p. 1. *Newspapers.com*. Accessed 2018.

"Terrible Accident on a New Jersey Railroad." *The Palmyra Spectator* [Palmyra, MO], 20 8 1880, p. 1. *Newspapers.com*. Accessed 2018.

"Testimony of Engineer." *The Philadelphia Inquirer* [Philadelphia], 8 1880.

"Thirteen Deaths." *The Ogden Junction* [Ogden, UT], 18 8 1880, p. 1. *Newspapers.com*. Accessed 2018.

Thompson, Maria. *Wawa*. Charleston, SC, Arcadia Publishing, 2004.

Trench, William S. *Realities of Irish Life*. Boston, Forgotten Books, 1880.

Watson, William E. *Massacre at Duffy's Cut*. Charleston, SC, The History Press, 2018.

Watts, J. F. *The Irish Americans*. Philadelphia, Chelsea House Publishers, 1996.

"A Whitewash Verdict." *National Republican* [Washington DC], 14 8 1880, p. 1. *Newspapers.com*. Accessed 2018.

"Whose Fault?" *The Philadelphia Inquirer* [Philadelphia], 18 8 1880, p. 1. *Newspaper.com*. Accessed 2018.

Wood, Julianna R. *Biographical Sketch of Richard D. Wood*. vol. II, Philadelphia, Forgotten Books, 1874. 3 vols.

Wood, Julianna R. *Biographical Sketch of Richard D Wood*. vol. I, Philadelphia, Forgotten Books, 1874. 3 vols.

Wood, Julianna R. *Biographical Sketch of Richard D. Wood*. vol. III, Philadelphia, Forgotten Books, 1874. 3 vols.

Made in the USA
Columbia, SC
14 August 2021